GW01605974

Edited by Samantha Lee
Designed by Yong Wen Yeu

Published in Singapore
by Epigram Books.
www.epigrambooks.sg

National Library Board, Singapore
Cataloguing-in-Publication Data

Tan, Christopher, 1972- author.
NerdBaker : extraordinary recipes,
stories & baking adventures from
a true oven geek / Christopher Tan.
Singapore : Epigram Books, 2015.

ISBN : 978-981-46-1577-8 (paperback)
ISBN : 978-981-46-1576-1 (ebook)

First edition, April 2015.
Third printing, September 2019.

CHRISTOPHER TAN

With warmest wishes for amazing baked goods!

NERDBAKER

EXTRAORDINARY RECIPES, STORIES & BAKING ADVENTURES
FROM A TRUE OVEN GEEK

E

EPIGRAM
SINGAPORE • LONDON

CONTENTS

FOREWORD

In the early 2000s, while researching a cookbook-cum-memoir, I made umpteen trips to Southeast Asia. I had heard from food guru colleagues that there was a journalist in Singapore who really, really knew his stuff. I emailed to propose we meet. "Raffles Place train station, just outside the turnstiles," he returned. "I'll be the chubby Asian guy in glasses"—a characteristically self-deprecating description that helped me spot Chris immediately. We ended up eating far more than we had good reason to. As we sat there, I could tell we'd be friends for life.

Since then, I've discovered that every encounter with Chris is an uncommon adventure in food.

When I was putting together an article on pandan, a beloved Southeast Asian aromatic leaf that's underappreciated elsewhere, I travelled to Singapore to seek Chris' help. We started at Tekka Market in Little India, where, he'd forewarned, the particular variety of pandan he'd specially ordered was gigantic. I was expecting big leaves. I wasn't expecting them to be nine feet long. We bought a sheaf, along with regular pandan and all sorts of sweet and savoury dishes that used pandan as a flavouring. We somehow convinced a taxi driver that we could get these monstrous tropical leaves and all this food into his car. At my hotel, we made it past the front desk to my room, where we photographed all of it. Then we ate what we could. And then we ate some more. By the end, we had created this phenomenal, nestlike mess—a foodie take on the kind of disarray rock stars used to leave their hotel rooms in. It took at least five increasingly hilarious calls to housekeeping before someone was willing to cart our pandan jungle away. I was a bit put out. Chris, having feasted, was in heaven.

The Chris that you, too, will get to know through this intensely personal, incredibly useful book is one of the most fervent food lovers on any continent. His expertise in Southeast Asian cuisines can fairly be called obsessive, but what sets him apart is his exploratory knowledge of so many of the world's cooking traditions—he's lived and travelled all over the globe.

A passionate home baker and cooking teacher, he seems to me a kind of food whisperer, divining after one bite what a particular dish is all about, what went into its creation, and what its influences are.

His culinary intelligence, generous spirit and exquisite sensitivity to provenance fills these pages, whose deep-dives into such diverse dishes as a classic French boule, a Japanese curry bread, and, yes, a Portuguese pandan pão de deus, explode what you thought you knew about baking while stoking your appetite, your imagination and your desire to cook.

—James Oseland, editor-in-chief, *Rodale's Organic Life*, and author of *Cradle of Flavor*

INTRODUCTION

Why do I bake?

I am the child of many ovens. My family oven, for which I helped my grandma prep hundreds of Lunar New Year cookies, in which my mother would bake kue lapis legit that steadily, stripily rose in its tin, layer by fragrant layer. The oven of my childhood neighbour Mrs Chong, whose amazing pies and curry puffs I could smell from over the fence. The oven of our small suburban bakery, which in the 1970s was all about custard puffs, chocolate-riced rum balls and how many plastic ornaments one could possibly cram onto a thickly buttercreamed birthday cake. Rather more posh hotel bakery ovens—how I miss the Marco Polo Cake Shop's strawberry tarts and hot cross buns. The oven at Yaohan department store, rolling out red bean anpan buns for ravenous hordes.

As a kid, I was picky about vegetables and spices, but vacuumed up any starchy thing not nailed down—pancakes, biscuits, buns without end... I was omnicarbivorous. My food world expanded after I moved to London with my family in my early teens. To ease the culture shock, I inhaled books, TV, music and more books. When not in bookshops, I sought solace at supermarkets, where ingredients abounded in a variety I'd never before seen, even staples like sugars and flours. And the milk! The milkman—a nursery-rhyme abstraction now made real—left our glass bottle order on the doorstep every morning, contents encoded by its foil cap: blue was skimmed (yuk), striped blue semi-skimmed, red normal, silver richer, gold top the best of

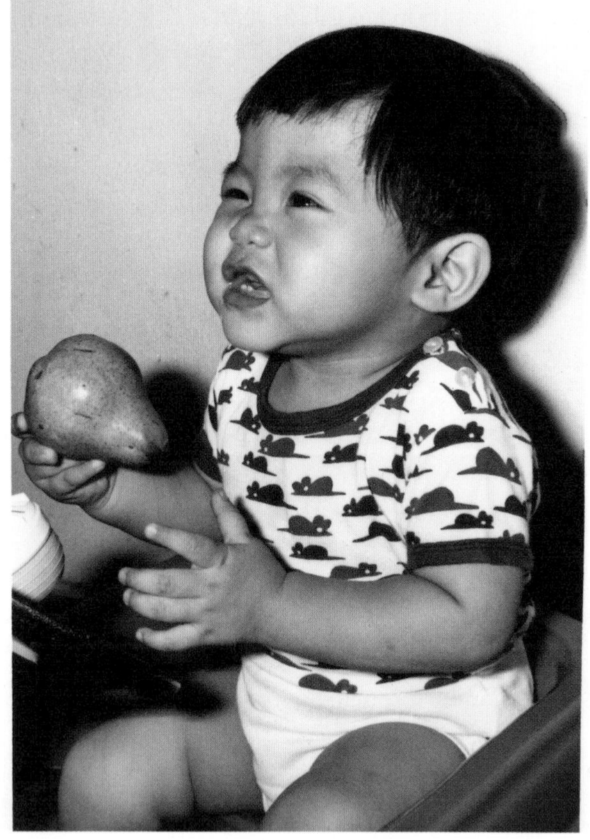

Clearly the pear was unstatisfactory.

all, an inch of thick cream floating at its zenith. Baked into custards and quiches, it made my awkward teenage phase more palatable, if no less awkward.

At high school, the cool kids went in for drama, covert smoking and doing everything ironically, even walking. I dove deep into biology, chemistry and advanced maths by day, and churned out chocolate roulades by night. I went on to study psychology at university, a fact which surprises many people until I point out that baking is the most affordable form of therapy there is. (Had you asked me "What's your major?" I would have replied, "Kenwood.") The healing regimen I inflicted on university mates included pizza, lasagna, pies, naan, and once (but never again), baked Alaska for 40 people. I learnt a lot in those years, less from the hits than from the misses, like the blueberry-orange sticky buns at which a friend exclaimed "Oh these are so nice!", followed by "They smell just like *soap*!... but really nice soap!"

After graduation, my writing job at a food magazine afforded me a grounding in European baking's formal rules, as well as a ringside seat for how chefs had started breaking them.

I hung out at professional pastry competitions and interviewed mad geniuses who electrified audiences with their command of the whisk.

I watched the dividing walls between modern patisserie, performance art and high-tech engineering stretch as thin as filo. I also sat at the feet of traditional cooks, and began collecting old recipe texts for their time-tested perspectives. I became more determined to improve the rigour and artfulness of my home baking.

Eventually I went freelance, which let me balance writing stints with teaching, speaking and penning cookbooks. And the bake goes on.

In today's culinary ecosystem, home cooks look to chefs for inspiration and trend cues, while chefs look to other chefs and farmers. However, in old cookbooks and memoirs, I glimpse eras when home cooks drove a lot of innovation, when some of the most interesting, creative gastronomy happened in private. I believe the tide is slowly turning that way again. Hobby bakers are reclaiming the home kitchen as fertile ground, now with blogs, social media and even reality shows to make their efforts visible. I salute them. They are my tribe.

It's important to me to stand on my tribal inheritance as an Asian and a Singaporean, too. Informing my baking with traditional Asian culture always leads me in fruitful directions. Yet I see so many cooks eagerly grasping the latest cheffy trends from abroad and adopting them wholesale, rather than unearthing their own roots for inspiration (which ironically is what often motivates their foreign chef heroes). Why hyperventilate about the 'molecular' method of spherification, when cendol—a starch gel set with controlled temperature and pH conditions, if you want to get technical—is a similar, equally riff-worthy recipe that was there all along? Of course, it's not about whose foodway is more correct or more 'authentic'

(a word by now bled dry from wanton use). It's about looking for greener grass at home as well as elsewhere; about viewing traditions not as fetters, but as rich soil in your own backyard, deep and firm enough to anchor and nurture your growth.

A friend once told me of how he went on a getaway to have lunch at England's The Fat Duck, only to be seated near three tables of Singaporeans, instantly identifiable by their chatter. The anecdote illustrates two things: we get around, and we have distinctive accents. Likewise, Singaporean baking is an exuberantly cosmopolitan tradition, yet with a style all its own. Our status as a port, former colonial outpost and immigrant hub has left a legacy of multiple official languages and gastronomies, and freewheeling eating habits. We cross many borders and tour many cultures within a single day's or hour's noshing, and think nothing of it. Doing likewise when I bake comes as naturally to me as breathing.

There are many fine books out there that will hone your skills on excellent classics, but my mission is to offer you new ideas and different paths into the grand world of baking.

We live in an age of recipe glut, where a single finger swipe accesses dozens of tutorials or orders a hundred cookbooks. But just as a writer can cook up a novel of startling freshness with the same words we use every day, so too a baker can use familiar ingredients to express new and striking thoughts, create an original narrative. This book is mine.

Why bake?

Baking is fun. Indeed, I think it's the most fun you can have with an apron on.

Baking is a craft. The more time you spend on it, the better you get at it. Expertise grows with rehearsal and experience—that's how craftspersons become artisans.

Baking is also an art (try denying this to anyone who's successfully made a croquembouche for the first time, and you will get smacked down), one whose works are easy to access and consume, in all senses.

Baking is meaningful and emotionally satisfying. More than just self-expression, it is elevated by the participation of others. It can strengthen our ties to our own and others' traditions, and our bonds with other people.

Baking focuses you. In many baked recipes, the methodical flow of preparation steps encourages a focus of mind, and a connection of mind and hand, that can be both soothing and energising. Pardon the spa-speak, but it's totally true.

Baking teaches you virtues, such as patience (laminated pastry), foresight (rustic bread), alertness (cookies burning in the oven!), precision (everything) and generosity (you gonna eat all those doughnuts yourself?). And faith: you trust in your preparation, close the oven door and pray. This is not even a metaphor.

Baking things yourself is good for you. Industrial baked goods often rely on extremes of taste and richness to hook our attention and create unworthy cravings. When you hold the reins, you can showcase aromas, flavours and textures first, and return sugar, salt and fat to their proper places. Your body will thank you for it.

Baking is not difficult. It truly isn't. If you can read and follow a sequence of instructions closely, you can bake.

What you won't find in this book

- The use of weird additives or flavour enhancers. I do not believe these are ever needed.
- Recipes created chiefly for speed, convenience or ease. Some of them are indeed fast and easy, but that is never their main point. Deliciousness is, always and every time. I want to show you how to cook with care and attention, not merely assemble prefab items.
- A restaurant-led perspective. I am a self-taught home baker—I use ingredients and equipment within the compass of a home cook with a decent kitchen, and access to physical and online baking supply stores and supermarkets.
- Secrecy. In my day job, I have had to read, road test, review and edit a lot of cookbooks, so I know how infuriating it is when recipes omit essential details or precision. I have tried my best to give you all the info you need for success.

How to use this book

- Read the opening chapters first, particularly the notes on ingredients, equipment and baking conditions. All these things differ for readers in different locations, and so I have described what I work with, to help you adjust the recipes and their requirements to your own circumstances.
- Read each recipe through a few times before embarking on it, so you get familiar with its logic and flow, and are not caught unawares by waiting times or equipment needs. This will save you from last-minute dashes to the shops, or having to abandon a half-made recipe for want of a crucial element.
- The first time around, make a recipe exactly as written. If you start altering it to your whim from the very beginning, you will not properly appreciate its original intention and its intended form. Get to know it first, and freestyle all you want afterwards.
- Bring this book into the kitchen with you, dog-ear the pages, annotate and splatter and stain them, love them into ragged-edgedness.

WITH GREAT BAKING COMES GREAT RESPONSIBILITY. USE YOUR POWERS FOR GOOD.

INGREDIENT & METHOD GUIDE

INGREDIENTS

WHEAT FLOURS

I use bleached **plain flour** (all-purpose flour) with 11 per cent protein. I use unbleached **bread flours** which vary from 13 to 15 per cent protein: the higher-protein ones work best for large but very light breads, like Chocolate Toddy Bread (page 58) and the giant doughnuts (page 132). I use bleached, finely milled **cake flour** with 7.5 to 8 per cent protein. **For any recipe, try to match the protein content of the specified flour for the best results.**

For wholewheat (wholemeal) cakes, pastries and cookies, I use **wholewheat pastry flour**, with 10 per cent protein; for wholewheat breads I use **wholewheat plain flour**, with around 13 per cent protein; in wholewheat flatbreads or soft breads, I like stone-ground **atta (chapati flour)**, around 12 per cent protein, but lacking enough gluten strength for high-rising loaves.

As for **other flours** such as cornmeal, rye flour or multigrain flour blends (which may include malted flours, sunflower seeds and the like), I buy small quantities at a time, organic for preference, with far-off expiry dates, and use them up promptly.

RICE FLOURS

I use regular white **rice flour**, milled from long-grain or medium-grain rice, in kueh, and for dusting cookie moulds to prevent sticking. **Sticky rice flour** is milled from medium- to short-grain sticky rice (also called glutinous rice, though it does not contain gluten protein). It comes in white and black types, the latter milled from black (a.k.a. purple) sticky rice.

Store all flours in cool, dry, airtight containers. All wholegrain flours should ideally be stored in the fridge or freezer, as they are more perishable.

STARCHES

Tapioca starch produces soft and elastic textures and shiny appearances in kueh recipes; it is also a good binding agent in doughs and batters. **Cornstarch** is an all-purpose thickener that also yields fine-grained, melt-in-the mouth textures in cakes and cookies. (**Custard powder** is mostly finely milled cornstarch.) **Potato starch** helps to produce coarse, fluffy, tender textures in breads and cakes and has a very neutral flavour. **Wheat starch** is essentially wheat flour with the protein removed, used often in dim sum for translucent dumpling skins, and as a thickener. **Water chestnut starch** is quite granular out of the box, and may need to be crushed finer for use. A strong thickener, it becomes slightly elastic and translucent when cooked with liquid. Most Asian supermarkets and baking supply stores sell all the above.

SUGARS

I use a fine granulation of **white sugar** for most purposes, and **caster sugar** (superfine sugar) for some creamed batters or meringues, as it dissolves faster. **Icing sugar** (confectioner's sugar) contains a bit of cornstarch to ward off clumping—it works well for garnishing, in glazes and in fine-textured cookies.

When I need brown sugar, I use **muscovado sugar** (unrefined cane sugar) as it has oodles more flavour than the molasses-tinted white sugar sold as regular 'brown sugar'.

Palm sugar, crystallised palm flower sap, is less sweet than cane sugar, with mineral, earth and umami notes. Palm sugars of varied hues, textures and flavour depths are produced across Southeast Asia and South Asia.

Syrups like molasses, treacle, golden syrup, honey and maple syrup lend flavour and moistness to baked goods, and help crusts to colour.

BUTTER, FAT & DAIRY

I prefer **unsalted butter** for all recipes, so I can control how much salt goes into them—except for a few traditional recipes which need the slightly stronger taste of salted butter. European-style butters made from cultured cream have more complex flavours. **Low-moisture butter**, with 82 to 84 per cent fat as opposed to regular butter's 80 to 82 per cent fat, is great for pastry and laminated doughs, as it softens more slowly and makes them easier to handle. I use sunflower **oil** for its neutral aroma.

To wet-render **pork**, **beef**, **lamb** or **chicken fat**, combine 3 to 4 parts finely diced or coarsely ground pure fat with 1 part water (by volume) in a heavy-based saucepan. Cover tightly and set over medium-low heat. The water will simmer and the fat will start to melt. When the water has mostly evaporated, check the fat—if some is still unmelted, add more water and continue to cook the mixture, covered, stirring often. When nearly all the fat has melted, open the lid a crack so any remaining water can evaporate. Once it has done so and the sizzling has ceased, leaving cracklings bobbing in liquid fat, strain off the fat with a fine-mesh metal sieve. The browner the cracklings get, the more toasted and less neutral the flavour of the rendered fat. Store the cooled fat in an airtight jar in the fridge or freezer.

I use full-cream **milk**, **yoghurt** and **condensed milk**, and whipping **cream** with 33 to 35 per cent fat.

Milk powder adds protein and flavour (and fat, if full-cream) to doughs. Sold at baking supply shops, milk powder treated specially for bread-making is high-heat-processed to dissolve faster and yield a higher rise. It is not the same as instant creamer or baby formula.

LEAVENING AGENTS

I use two types of instant yeast, **regular instant yeast** and **osmotolerant instant yeast**, both sold at baking supply shops, good supermarkets or online. Osmotolerant yeast (such as Bruggeman Brown or SAF Gold) thrives in enriched or sweetened doughs which would make regular yeast sluggish, but I find it works fine in regular doughs too. If you can only get instant yeast in large packs, transfer a few months' supply to an airtight jar and keep it in the fridge; seal, double-bag and stash the rest in the freezer. I seldom use fresh or frozen yeast simply because I cannot usually get either.

Between **single-acting baking powder** and **double-acting baking powder**, the latter acts over a longer time period, yielding a better overall rise, and is my first choice. The former is fine if that's all you have. Store baking powder in cool, airtight conditions and refresh your supply every few months.

Bicarbonate of soda reacts with acidic ingredients (brown sugar, vinegar, fruit juice) to produce a leavening effect. It also helps cakes and cookies to brown, but can result in a soapy, bitter flavour if used in excess.

Ammonium bicarbonate (a.k.a. baker's ammonia or chow fun), traditional to both Western and Asian baking, produces light, crispy, crunchy, crackled textures. Typically used only in cookies, as the gaseous ammonia it produces during baking is most easily driven off from small or thin items.

OTHER INGREDIENTS

The mineral content of **water** can affect other flavours. If your tap water is very hard or has a non-neutral taste, filter it before use. Boil highly chlorinated water to drive the chlorine off.

I use **eggs** weighing 60 g each (in the shell) for all recipes.

I use fine sea **salt** with no additives.

Coconut milk is of course best when home-squeezed from freshly grated mature coconut, but the latter is getting scarce even in urbanised Asia. Best substitutes in order of decreasing preference: ready-squeezed chilled coconut milk, canned coconut milk, long-life coconut cream diluted as needed.

Buy **spices**, **nuts**, **nut flours**, and **seeds** in small quantities from a shop with high turnover, keep them in a dry, cool place—ideally the freezer, or the coldest fridge shelf—and use them up quickly. Store **nut and seed pastes** in the fridge. Chill **flavour extracts** like vanilla and rose water too—all-natural ones will serve you best.

Taste gourmet **chocolate** next to cheaper options, and you'll see that the good stuff is smoother, more intense, and far more worth the price. Save the dearest and most complex chocs for eating neat, but don't ruin a recipe with the cheapest common denominator. Take note of cacao percentages, which indicate how much of the chocolate consists of pure cacao bean. I typically opt for 60 to 80 per cent chocolates.

Most supermarket **cocoa powder** has been Dutch-processed with alkali, which deepens its colour and flavour. **Natural cocoa powder**, usually labelled as such, has a paler, foxy hue and lighter taste, but the lack of alkaline processing plays up its fruity and acidic notes. As with chocolate, higher quality is worth the price, for either kind. **Cacao nibs** are chopped-up cacao beans—check the label to see if they've been roasted or sweetened.

Cream of tartar, an acid salt extracted from winemaking residues, stabilises beaten egg whites, and reacts with bicarbonate of soda to effect leavening.

Baking spray is a mix of oil, flour, lecithin to aid browning and prevent sticking, and propellants. It is sprayed onto pans to help baked cakes release easily. I use it on pans with complicated shapes, and for speed's sake in large-batch baking. Otherwise, greasing and flouring pans is enough.

EQUIPMENT

In each recipe I have explicitly listed essential equipment. I have assumed most cooks own basic items such as: rolling pins, mixing bowls, spatulas, plain baking trays, a pastry brush, tea towels, plastic wrap, foil and such.

The single most important thing you can do to improve your baking and make it more consistent is to start measuring by weight.

Measuring by volume introduces a margin of error, because the volumes of dry ingredients always vary depending on how they have been stored, transported, treated or transferred into measuring cups. As with fashion, so with baking—volumes can be compacted or fluffed up, but the scales never lie. Investing in an accurate **digital weighing scale** is never a waste. (To convert grams to ounces, divide by 28.) I do use **metal measuring spoons** for small ingredient quantities.

It is important to know your **oven**, its hot spots or other idiosyncrasies. Monitor its temperature accuracy during baking by hanging a dial-type oven thermometer from a rack. Fan assistance improves heat circulation and may reduce baking times, but is not always needed. Most items bake best on the middle shelf, unless otherwise specified.

I can't do without my high-wattage, steel-goblet, made-in-India **blender/processor**, designed for that cuisine's constant grinding of spices and grains. It easily reduces dry spices to powders and fresh ones to pastes, turns nuts into flour and coarse sugar into superfine.

If you intend to bake more and bake often, invest in a **stand mixer**. It creams butter, kneads bread dough and does many other things that would exhaust a hand-held mixer, or hand. Brand allegiance can be as emotional as it is rational, so ask around, do your research and pick the model that suits your baking habits, kitchen space and price point.

I prefer **baking pans** and **baking sheets** with medium-grey finishes, whether metallic or non-stick, as darker finishes can over-brown crusts. Thicker metal conducts heat more evenly. I seldom use **silicone moulds**, as the material's insulating properties often result in unevenly browned crusts.

My **rolling pins**—long 50 cm ones for dough and pastry, short 15 cm ones for dim sum and small items—are wooden, save a heavy-weight plastic one for especially stiff doughs.

My favourite **spatula** is completely coated in high-temperature-tolerant silicone, the blade joining the handle seamlessly—great for stirring everything, and a cinch to clean. I also have **a wide-bladed, long-handled spatula** for large-batch mixing. For whisking egg whites or folding flour into egg foams, I use a **big balloon whisk**. I use **natural bristle pastry brushes** for glazing and brushing.

Stainless steel **cookie cutters** are easiest to maintain (plastic ones can build up greasy residue). A plastic or metal **dough scraper**, with one grippable edge and an opposite sharper edge for cutting, is indispensable for scooping, scraping, flipping and portioning dough. It should feel comfortable to hold, like an extension of your hand.

Use **food-safe plastic wrap** for wrapping uncooked doughs. I prefer to keep any kind of plastic wrap away from hot food, whatever labels say.

Proper non-stick **baking paper** will serve you better than thin, el cheapo tracing paper.

BAKING CONDITIONS

My kitchen's ambient **room temperature** hovers between 28 and 34°C, its **humidity** between 75 and 90 per cent. All the recipes were tested in this environment. If your kitchen is much cooler, expect yeast dough proofing times to lengthen. If your air is much drier, let loaves and buns proof in an enclosed, humid environment, like a closed oven with a bowl of hot water tucked in a corner. Also, store baked goods well wrapped so they don't dry out.

1.

OBSESSIONS, ADDICTIONS & ENDANGERED SPECIES

These subjects and recipes aren't necessarily the most white-knucklingly thrilling or the most appallingly decadent or even the most decorative in the book. But they are the ones on which I have gained the most weight and lost the most sleep, the ones I have tested to carb coma and back. (I have the stray burns to show for it.) They are the treasures which have stayed on my mind the longest, and back to which I always wander again and again. I love to bake them because I can tinker with and elaborate on them according to my mood. They are a pleasure—and a challenge, which is inseparable from the pleasure—to make. They are as much a part of me as my handwriting.

BUNHEAD

From bread I came, and to bread I will always return.

In my tweenhood, my self-propelled forays into the kitchen were rare at best. I was most happy just to eat, not cook. Then, when I was 14, while idly reading magazines lying around the house, I ran across a recipe for hot dinner rolls.

Entranced by the warmly lit, sharply angled photos (the 1980s, y'all) of shiny, golden, sesame-bedecked buns, I set forth to make them. Thus began my baking obsession, along with a season of boredom for my parents as I inflicted humdrum rolls on them repeatedly for weeks.

I have lived my life with floury hands ever since. As my baking repertoire expanded, so did the transient fixations. Marble cake one month, choux buns the next, followed by Scotch pancakes, chicken pie, kue ambon...but I find myself constantly drawn back to breads. It's something about working with yeast, perhaps—each bake is a collaboration, not a monologue; grown, not just made. I think this is why so many of the expert bread bakers I've met have been generous, easy-going, nurturing people—they know their success rests on the sloping shoulders of several million tiny friends.

MAKES 15 OR 16 ROLLS

INGREDIENTS

230 g	water
100 g	diced, peeled potato
75 g	caster sugar
30 g	milk powder
1 tsp	salt
2	egg yolks
2	egg whites
500 g	bread flour
2 tsp	osmotolerant or regular instant yeast (page 15)
50 g	unsalted butter, cubed and softened
	oil and butter, for greasing and brushing

EQUIPMENT

- a stand mixer fitted with the dough hook
- a deep 25 cm round cake tin

CHRIS' HOT ROLLS

My rolls have since improved.

Asians like soft breads. I don't think I'm being unfairly stereotypical. It's difficult to walk two blocks in downtown Singapore, Seoul or Tokyo without passing at least one bakery piled high with buns and small loaves. Some will likely be excellent versions of European breads, but most of the others will have softness as their central virtue. And I don't mean soft-as-compared-to-say-a-hearty-German-rye soft—I mean really soft. Princess-and-the-Pea-feather-mattress soft. Scary soft. Bordering on evanescent soft.

Some commercial bakeries doubtlessly achieve these textures with dough 'improvers', conditioners and other additives I'd rather not think about. But the home baker needs no inscrutable powders to make plush, cushiony breads, as this recipe demonstrates. It showcases three techniques which I use often in my kitchen and throughout this book: using potato to boost softness, lightness and shelf life; hydrating and pre-cooking a small portion of the dough's starch (the potato, in this case), which also promotes a softer texture; and short bursts of kneading alternated with short rests, an old French practice described by famed baker Raymond Calvel in his book *The Taste of Bread*.

Together, they allow me to make the hot rolls of my dreams, three decades on. Tender, light and 'shreddy'—which means you can easily pull their crumb apart into long, airy shreds—these have personality beyond their softness.

POINTERS

- Use a floury textured potato for the best results. Waxy textured varieties won't disintegrate as readily.
- The knead-rest-knead-rest-knead sequence builds structure in the dough without overworking it, which is good for flavour. You can knead it with your hands, in which case alternate 2-minute kneadings with the 5-minute rests—use a dough scraper to help you knead, to avoid incorporating too much extra flour into the dough.
- As you shape the buns, the dough should feel silky, springy and alive under your fingers, as if it can't wait to slip the surly bonds of earth and surge for the heavens. It should stick to your oiled fingers and work surface just enough to assist in shaping—that is, hardly at all.
- These are generously-sized rolls. If you wish, make them smaller, but place them in a pan of such size that they crowd together—this close snuggling encourages them to rise up high before they set, yielding the airy, shreddy crumb.

- Don't cut them apart or in half—tear them with your hands to enjoy their texture.
- Store buns in a resealable plastic bag at cool room temperature or in the fridge. They will stay fresh-tasting and soft for at least 3 to 4 days.
- I gave some of these rolls to a friend, who rang me the next day to report a Proustian moment: their aroma and flavour had unexpectedly "transported" her back to Dong Log Wee, a venerated and long-gone Hainanese bakery that once stood on Killiney Road in Singapore. I may not ever better that compliment.

METHOD

1 Combine water and diced potato in a small pot with a tight-fitting lid. Cover, bring to a boil over medium heat and cook for 10 to 12 minutes, until the potato is very soft.

2 Pour contents of pot into a mixing bowl. Add caster sugar, milk powder, salt and egg yolks, and whisk hard until the potato disintegrates and the dry ingredients dissolve, making a smooth mixture. Let it cool to room temperature.

3 Whisk egg whites into potato mixture, add bread flour and osmotolerant yeast, and stir with a spatula to make a rough dough. Cover bowl with a damp tea towel. Let dough rest for 30 minutes.

4 Knead dough on medium-low speed for 1 minute, then re-cover the bowl with the damp tea towel and let it rest for 5 minutes. Repeat the kneading and resting twice more. The dough should be elastic and smooth by this point.

5 Finally, add the butter to the bowl and knead until the dough absorbs it and starts to 'clean'—that is, pull away from—the bowl sides, which should take 1 to 2 minutes. Cover the bowl and let the dough stand at cool room temperature (page 17, Baking Conditions) until it has doubled in size, about 1 hour.

6 Lightly grease a work surface and your hands with oil. Turn dough out and gently deflate it with your

fingertips. Divide it into 15 or 16 balls, each weighing about 70 g. Cup each ball under your palm and fingers and drag it in small circles on the work surface, to compact and tighten it. Cover balls with a damp tea towel and let them rest for 10 minutes.

7 Grease cake tin with melted butter.

8 Flatten a ball slightly, then draw its edges together underneath the ball, so that its upper surface rounds and tightens. Pinch the underside firmly to seal the gathered edges, then repeat the cupping and dragging to neaten the ball. Shape all buns likewise. Tuck buns into greased tin, sealed sides down, snuggling them close together. Cover tin with an upturned mixing bowl and let buns rise until almost doubled, about 20 to 30 minutes.

9 Preheat oven to 180°C. Place a shelf in the middle position.

10 Brush buns with melted butter. Bake for 25 to 30 minutes, until risen and browned. If they darken quickly, cover them with foil. They are done when the middle bun sounds hollow and feels slightly springy when tapped with a fingertip.

11 Transfer tin to a rack to cool. Serve buns while still slightly warm, with lots of butter.

PAIN POILÂNE 1kg £3.2

BOULE OF BROKEN DREAMS

My first taste of sourdough bread didn't augur very well. I was 9 years old and on a family holiday. Exploring a San Francisco street market, we passed a lady selling baked goods. Stricken by her sad, grief-glazed eyes (which in hindsight may just have been rheumy), I pestered my parents to buy something to cheer her up.

The loaf looked more or less ordinary, but when I bit into its pale puffiness, it assaulted me. The dank, screechingly sour crumb set my tongue a-twang like a broken guitar string, and I had to spit it out.

Fortunately, my tastebuds grew up with me. Living near a largely Jewish suburb of London in my teens, I got to know crusty bloomer loaves, caraway-flecked light rye bread—so good folded around fat-rimmed salt beef—and bagels. Soho's patisseries taught me to love properly buttery-moist-flaky French croissants, and a quotidian baguette, a thing of beauty and joy for but a day. Crumb by crumb, I stocked my mental taste-library with malt, granary, rye, barley, oat, spelt.

My second truly formative sourdough experience came years later, when as a journo I interviewed Californian chef and bread guru Nancy Silverton, founder of La Brea Bakery and (since) co-founder of the Mozza restaurants. She gave me a seeded dill sourdough boule. It was authoritative-tasting, plangent, as complex as any fruit. I ate it slowly in one sitting, my eyes as wet as the sad market lady's,

because I did not know how life would go on after the last transcendent bite was swallowed and there was no more.

Somehow, it did. Years later still, I wandered into the London bakery of French bread demigod Lionel Poilâne, my byline known to no-one there, presented my business card to the mademoiselle at the counter, and asked if by any chance M. Poilâne was in and free for a chat. Miraculously, he was, and gifted me 20 minutes of his time and opinion with utmost kindness, even instructing a kitchen hand to show me the brick oven. The grace he showed to a gormless food writer has stayed with me more strongly than the heavenly taste of his bread. When I heard about his passing not long afterwards, my heart fell like an overproofed miche.

These two encounters pretty much sealed the deal. I wanted to make, to perfect, *to know* this kind of bread for myself. Over the next decade I sifted cookbooks, libraries and the internet for formulas and kneading methods and slash patterns. I made a litany of those at whose feet I yearned to sit: Silverton Reinhart Robertson Calvel Hensperger Leader Lahey Lepard. I parented wild yeast starters, struggling with months of late-night and early-morning feedings, constant cleaning up, and panicked cosseting, and all died of one thing or another. I baked loaf after cruddy loaf. Some smelt of alcohol, some were bricklike from over-kneading, others looked like fossilised dinosaur turds.

Eventually, the sun started to break through the clouds of flour, and I learned a few more things.

Backstage at Poilâne.

- Bread is something to break together with others. It's about gratitude and appreciation, not judgement against a perceived ideal.
- Breadmaking is as personal as any art, traced in flour and hydration ratios rather than pigments or tunings. You don't have to replicate some other baker's recipe down to the crumb-bubble diameter—it is enough to make bread which *you* like and enjoy.
- Every loaf is the product of many skill sets—yours, the miller's, the yeasts', the water authorities', the oven manufacturer's, the weatherman's. If wine has a terroir and oysters have a 'meroir', then bread has a faroir, a mainoir, a fouroir.* So every loaf will be unique. Don't sweat it. *Vive la différence*.
- If a loaf flops, it doesn't matter. Make breadcrumbs for the freezer. It's just flour and water, and if you think hard about what likely went wrong, you'll have learnt a lesson you can apply next time. Savour the process.

With these realisations, my breads improved, slowly. Doughs responded to my touch; loaves bloomed; crusts sang as they cooled. Previously opaque recipes suddenly cleared like a summer sky as I connected them to the goings-on in my mixing bowl and under my hands.

Decades on from that first spat-out sourdough, the perfect loaf is still somewhere beyond the horizon, where it will stay. I'm content to enjoy the landscape between here and there, smelling the wheat and roses along the way.

**mer = sea, farine = flour, main = hand, four = oven*

MAKES 1 MEDIUM LOAF

INGREDIENTS

Preferment

50 g	rye flour
50 g	wholewheat flour
⅛ tsp	instant yeast (page 15)
50 g	boiled and cooled water
1½ tbsp	plain unsweetened yoghurt, with live cultures

Dough

240 g	boiled and cooled water
1 tbsp	plain unsweetened yoghurt, with live cultures
½ tsp	instant yeast
250 g	unbleached bread flour
50 g	wholewheat bread flour
50 g	rye flour
50 g	multigrain flour blend (page 14), or more bread flour
50 g	warm water
10 g	fine sea salt
	oil, for greasing
	rice flour, for dusting

EQUIPMENT

- a round-bottomed colander or mixing bowl of around 1.5-litre capacity
- a heavy baking sheet, pizza pan, or roasting tin
- a large stainless-steel mixing bowl, which when inverted will sit flush on the baking sheet, with no gaps around the rim
- baking paper
- a sharp knife or baker's lame blade, for slashing

CHRIS' RUSTIC BOULE

These are bread-baking accoutrements that I wish I had, but don't: a wood-fired oven; wicker bannetons to mould my loaves; a big fridge or cool-room space for slow, retarded proofing; a fancy baking stone; spare change for the electricity bill run up by hour-long preheats of said fancy baking stone; a big cast-iron Dutch oven; spare change for the chiropractic sessions occasioned by repeated lifting of said Dutch oven. Even if I could afford linen proofing basket liners, and French flour to rub into them, they'd probably accumulate dust mites and mould. I am, as I have said, a serial sourdough starter killer.

This is what I do have: a domestic oven; a small Asian fridge packed to the gills; regular equipment found in most kitchens or a good kitchenware shop. With these I can make decent bread, and you can, too. This recipe is a mash-up of everything I've learnt about bread over the years, inspired by all the loaves I've loved. It isn't true sourdough, but it is sturdy and delicious. I've spelt everything out in fine detail for those of you not yet comfortable with the improvisation and serendipity that bread-making ultimately invites us to. May this further you on your own bread adventure.

METHOD

1 Make the preferment. Mix all ingredients together into a small ball of dough, stirring it to mop up all the dry flour—it need not be perfectly even. Place it in a clean bowl or container that can hold at least twice the volume of the dough ball. Cover with plastic wrap or a lid. Refrigerate for 12 to 16 hours. It will roughly double in size.

2 Make the dough. Combine preferment, water and yoghurt in a large mixing bowl and whisk until the preferment breaks up into small clumpy bits. Stir in yeast, bread flour, wholewheat bread flour, rye flour and multigrain flour blend, to make a shaggy dough. Cover the bowl with a plate, and let it stand at cool room temperature for 30 minutes.

3 Stir lukewarm water and salt together until salt dissolves. Pour salt water evenly over dough. With wet hands, gently pull a flap of the dough to stretch it out a little, towards the rim of the mixing bowl, then fold it back towards the dough's centre. Rotate the bowl 45 degrees. Grab a new corner of the dough and repeat the stretching, folding and rotating, for a total of about 14 to 18 stretches and folds, by which time the dough should have mostly absorbed the salt water. It will be sticky. Cover the bowl again and let it stand for 45 minutes at cool room temperature.

4 With wet hands, stretch and fold the dough again, 8 to 10 times. Flip dough upside down so its smooth underside faces up. Cover and let stand for 45 minutes.

(continued on the next page)

Risen preferment

Dough after first stretch-fold session

Dough after fourth and final stretch-fold session

Boule after final proof, in colander

Slashed boule

Finished boule

5 With wet hands, stretch and fold the dough again, 8 to 10 times. Flip dough upside down. Cover and let stand for 45 minutes.

6 With wet hands, stretch and fold the dough again, 8 to 10 times. Flip dough upside down. Cover and let stand for 30 minutes.

7 Rub work surface and your hands with oil, but lightly—the dough should not slide around freely between them, as you need some friction to assist in its shaping.

8 Scrape the dough out onto the work surface. Cup your hands around the side of the dough furthest from you, and draw your hands towards yourself, dragging the dough along the board. It should tighten and plump up as it resists the motion. Rotate the dough 90 degrees clockwise and repeat, then rotate and drag 4 to 6 times more. The dough should now be a neat round ball. Cover it with the upturned mixing bowl and let it relax undisturbed for 20 minutes.

9 Rub or spray a round-bottomed colander or bowl with oil. Dust it with a thin, even coat of rice flour.

10 Uncover the dough ball. Flip it upside down. Flatten it very gently with your fingertips. Grab its near edge and stretch it gently towards you, then fold it back towards the centre, covering the middle third of the dough and leaving the top third exposed. Repeat this stretching and folding with the left and right sides, then finally the edge farthest from you, bringing that all the way to the edge nearest you. Flip the dough upside down. Repeat the cupping, dragging and rotating that you did earlier, so that the loaf forms a ball with a smooth upper surface and its seams bunched together on its underside.

11 Quickly dust some rice flour evenly over the shaped loaf. Pick up the loaf and place it upside down in the prepared colander or bowl, so that its smooth top is in the bottom of the bowl and its underside now faces up. If any seams threaten to gape, pinch them firmly. Cover the colander with an upturned mixing bowl. Let it stand at cool room temperature until the loaf has risen to just slightly less than twice its original size, which could take anywhere from 30 to 50 minutes.

12 Place a shelf in the bottom third of the oven, and a heavy baking sheet or pizza pan on top of it. Preheat the oven to 220°C. Time this so that it reaches temperature about 10 minutes before the dough is ready to be turned out, so the sheet gets good and hot. Have ready your large stainless steel mixing bowl.

13 Uncover the colander. Place a sheet of baking paper on top of the colander, and a chopping board on top of that. Holding both colander and chopping board securely, invert both together. Lift off the colander—the dough should release cleanly onto the paper. With a very sharp knife or lame blade, slash the dough as you wish (see Pointers).

14 Open the oven. Slide the sheet of paper and loaf together off the chopping board and onto the hot baking sheet. Immediately cover the loaf with the stainless steel mixing bowl. Shut the oven door. Bake for 20 minutes.

15 Open the oven. Use a spatula to lift up an edge of the mixing bowl, grab the bowl in your oven-gloved hand, and lift it off the baking sheet, exposing the risen but pale loaf. Shut oven door. Bake boule for 25 to 30 minutes more, until deeply browned, and it sounds hollow when tapped with a finger.

16 Transfer the baking sheet to a rack. Let stand for 5 minutes, then slide the loaf off the sheet onto the rack, so air can circulate around it. Let it cool. Try to resist cutting into it until it is lukewarm, as it needs to set into its final texture—though who am I to talk, I usually can't wait that long. Eat with lots of butter.

POINTERS

- See page 14 for more information about the flours.
- The equipment I use: a plastic Japanese colander about 22 cm in diameter and 10 cm deep; a heavy polished-aluminium pizza tray, about 3 mm thick and 33 cm in diameter; a heavy stainless steel mixing bowl about 28 cm in diameter and 18 cm deep; a baker's lame or a paring knife.
- Live yoghurt adds flavour—the yeast cells cavort with their lactobacilli friends—and the milk proteins enhance crust colour.
- The proofing timings stated above work out right for my tropic-temperature kitchen. Expect slightly different timings if your kitchen is much warmer or cooler. (See page 17.)
- The dough is very moist, but will not stick to wet hands. With each subsequent set of stretches and folds, it will become softer, more elastic, more airy and spongy-feeling, and pull away more cleanly from the bowl sides.
- Treat the dough gently. Stretching and folding lends it strength and structure in a more controllable, nurturing way than violent slapping or punching.
- When the dough has finished its fermentation and is ready for shaping, it will feel lively—puffy, springy, resilient. With experience, you will learn to discern this by feel.
- Rice flour prevents the dough from sticking to the colander or bowl.
- A colander's holes allow the skin of the shaped loaf to breathe and dry out slightly as it proofs. This helps it to keep its shape when it is turned out, and also yields a slightly thicker crust. Using an unperforated bowl instead results in a thinner crust.
- To slash the dough, hold the blade at a sharp angle to the dough surface. Picture in your mind how the slashes will look, overlay your mental picture on your view of the loaf, then trace the pattern with the blade tip, moving swiftly and decisively, slashing about 6 mm to 7 mm deep. Slow or hesitant slashing with the blade edge inevitably ends in raggedy snagging and dragging.
- Do not let the slashed loaf wait around. Hustle it into the oven.
- The heavy baking sheet or pizza pan soaks up heat during the oven preheating, then transmits it to the loaf, giving it 'oven spring'—a rapid initial rise that opens up the slashes.
- Baking the loaf under the metal mixing bowl traps the steam that it gives off. The resulting humid environment helps it rise to its maximum extent before it sets, and produces a shiny, beautiful crust.
- The finished boule's dark, burnished crust colour translates to a deeper, more caramelised, toasty flavour.
- Store this bread in a brown paper bag at cool room temperature. It will keep for 3 to 5 days. It freezes well for several weeks, if tightly wrapped.

NO FILTERS

The night was warm.

We arrived at the flat one by one, heading straight to the kitchen to unpack and heat up our bounty. Glass beads dangling from a lamp shivered, sending globules of light spangling across the wall. Invisible swirls of vaporised oil curled through the air, coating our hair and skin with the aroma of unspecified meat.

We milled around, making nervous small talk. We'd chosen the theme for this dinner—one of our gang's regular potlucks—weeks ago, and had been discussing what we'd cook ever since. We'd carefully built the necessary mental reserves of grit and commitment. As the risks of our endeavour loomed ever closer, however, the vision changed and shifted, revealing fissures of doubt in our initial bravado. But what is man without a challenge? What is life without a frisson of uncertainty, of danger? What is a meal without the lurking promise of antacids?

This was the menu:

SPAKORAS
Spam fritters in a spicy Indian-inspired chickpea flour batter

RAVIOLI FRITTI DI ZUCCA E MISTERIO DE MAIALE
Fried Spam and pumpkin dumplings

SPOTCH EGGS
Hard-boiled eggs cloaked in mashed Spam, breadcrumbed and fried

SPAM AND POTATO CURRY
A dry curry garnished with fresh coriander

SPAM AND POTATO CUTLETS
Pan-fried cakes of Spam and mashed potato

SPAM ROTI JOHN
French loaf topped with mashed Spam and beaten egg, and pan-fried

FRESH TOMATO CHUTNEY
To cleanse the palate between bites of Spam

SPAM AND PINEAPPLE UPSIDE-DOWN CAKE

SPAKLAVA
Baklava with walnuts, almonds and bits of crispy-fried Spam

We gasped, ate, laughed—not a little hysterically—talked, ate some more, reclined like banquet-addled Romans. We moaned softly as digestion began. We—I—lived to tell this tale, but only just.

SERVES 8 TO 12 INTREPID PEOPLE

INGREDIENTS

Topping

2 cans	luncheon meat (about 700 g)
4	fresh or canned pineapple rings, well drained

Batter

160 g	plain unsweetened yoghurt
50 g	water
½ tsp	salt
115 g	fine cornmeal
130 g	plain flour
1½ tsp	baking powder
⅛ tsp	bicarbonate of soda
2	eggs
40 g	sugar
100 g	unsalted butter, melted

Caramel

90 g	unsalted butter
45 g	light brown sugar

EQUIPMENT

- a round cookie cutter (see step 1)
- a 20 cm square cake pan

POINTERS

- Step 2 allows the cornmeal to hydrate more evenly, resulting in a more tender, less gritty texture.
- For a hint of teriyaki flavour and a darker finish, add a small splash of Japanese soy sauce to the caramel ingredients.
- Leftovers can be warmed up—wrap in foil and steam them, to keep the cornbread moist—and will taste even better and more lethal than you may imagine.

HULI ALA POHIHIHI PUA'A KALA KAHIKI KŪLINA PA'IPALAOA

SPAM AND PINEAPPLE UPSIDE-DOWN CORNBREAD CAKE

No prizes for guessing which two of the menu's dishes I came up with. Here's a recipe for one of them. It isn't as odd as you might think: the retro synergy of luncheon meat and pineapple is appealingly underlined by sweet-salty cornbread. Mahalo to my Hawaiian friends!

METHOD

1 Open the luncheon meat cans. Savour the *thhrruupppp* sound as the blocks slide out. Cut them into slices about 12 mm thick; you should have at least 4 slices. In a frying pan over medium heat, fry the slices until some of their fat has rendered and they have a light crust, about 5 minutes, turning them once. Drain slices on paper towels and let cool, then use a round cookie cutter to stamp out circles or rings the same size as the pineapple rings. Nibble furtively on the leftovers.

2 Start the batter. Whisk yoghurt, water, salt and cornmeal together in a large mixing bowl until smooth. Cover and set aside for 20 minutes.

3 Sift flour, baking powder and bicarbonate of soda together into a bowl, and whisk well to mix. Set aside.

4 Preheat oven to 180°C. Place a shelf in the middle position.

5 Assemble caramel and topping. Combine butter and brown sugar in a small pan and cook over medium-low heat until the butter has melted and the sugar has almost completely dissolved. Pour caramel into cake pan and spread it out evenly. Arrange pineapple and luncheon meat on top of caramel, filling any gaps with the trimmings.

6 Finish batter. Add eggs, sugar and melted butter to cornmeal mixture, and whisk until smooth and well blended. Add flour mixture and whisk well until incorporated. Scrape batter over the pineapple and luncheon meat, spreading it evenly.

7 Bake for 30 minutes, until cornbread is risen and golden, and a tester inserted into its centre—without going into the topping layer—comes out clean.

8 Remove pan from oven. Immediately, while caramel is still hot, run a sharp knife around the edge of the cake. Place serving plate upside down on top of pan. Holding pan and plate tightly together, invert them so the cake unmoulds onto the plate. Wait 1 minute for everything to ease and drip down, then lift off the pan. Serve warm.

EON MEAT / PAIN DE VIANDE
HIGH IN PROTEIN TENEUR ÉLEVÉE EN PROTÉINES
340 g

READY TO EAT LUNCHEON MEAT
PAIN DE VIANDE PRÊT À MANGER
OUR PREMIUM PORK NOTRE PORC DE CHOIX
340 g

LUNCHEON MEAT / PAIN DE

100% 제주산 돼지고기로 만든
탐라팜
순 돼지고기
(돼지고기함량 94.05% 중)
프레스햄(식육통조림) 340 g

SPAM
Luncheon Meat
TOCINO
LIMITED EDITION
Hormel Foods
NET WT 12 OZ (340g)

100% 제주산
롯데마트
통큰

READY TO EAT • PRÊT À MANGER
EON MEAT / PAIN DE VIANDE
HIGH IN PROTEIN TENEUR ÉLEVÉE EN PROTÉINES
340 g

MAPLE LEAF
Klik
READY TO EAT LUNCHEON MEAT
PAIN DE VIANDE PRÊT À MANGER
OUR PREMIUM PORK NOTRE PORC DE CHOIX
340 g

MAPLE LEAF
READY TO EAT • PRÊT À MANGER
LUNCHEON MEAT / PAIN DE

100% 제주산 돼지고기로 만든
탐라팜
순 돼지고기
(돼지고기함량 94.05% 중)

SPAM
Luncheon Meat
TOCINO
LIMITED EDITION

100% 제주산
롯데마트
통큰

LUNCHEON MEAT

Anyone comfortable with diverse meat textures and a certain sense of kitchen thrift—which is to say, most traditional cooks of any stripe—shouldn't feel fazed by canned luncheon meat. After all, it's a perfect nose-to-tail food: it might contain nose, it could include tail, who's to say?

Spam, probably the world's most famous luncheon meat, was created by the Hormel company and first sold in the US in 1937, touted as a handy, versatile convenience product. During and after World War II, it followed American GIs around the world in supply and aid packages, and quickly found a footing wherever it landed. So ubiquitous has it since become that its trademarked name has become colloquial shorthand for any kind of canned forcemeat.

Luncheon meat's hyperseasoned savour is best complemented by bland carbs, one of the reasons why Spam has naturalised itself so inextricably across Asia. One of my favourite meals as a kid (and, frankly, ever) was white rice, fried Spam and fried egg. A similar collation is dear to Filipinos, who call it spamsilog ('si' from sinangag, garlic fried rice, 'log' from itlog, fried egg). At Hong Kong's cha chaan tengs (tea restaurants), luncheon meat is a staple partner for toast, noodles, rice and buns. Singaporean stalls hawking fried breakfast noodles invariably offer fried luncheon meat to further gild the greasy lily.

Spam is hugely popular in Korea, where it has been joined on supermarket shelves by home-grown luncheon meat brands, flavoured with onion, cheese, garlic, beef and such. The Philippines has Tocino Spam, named for and seasoned like a sweetened cured pork dish—in fact it tastes rather like Taiwanese sausage, its mystery meat cousin. In Singapore, circular orange cans of Ma Ling pork luncheon meat probably have the most devotees, though one can also find meats made from mutton (tastes like doner kebab), chicken (looks like a section of a giant chicken frankfurter), beef (mmm, astronaut burgers), even fish (surprisingly, not bad).

One of the most sublime creations of all time in the Spam-and-rice genre is Hawaiian-Japanese: the Spam musubi, a fried Spam slice laid atop a sushi rice cake, girdled with a nori seaweed strip. Fancy cooks use special moulds to compact the rice to the right dimensions; hardcore traditionalists use the empty Spam can, with both ends removed. Made either way, Spam musubi rocks.

STICK FIGURES

As a youngster thrown around by the turbulence of late adolescence, I would often reach—as one might for aspirin, or a lifejacket—for a dog-eared paperback, one of those chance bookshop discoveries that changes your life. *The Pillow Book of Sei Shônagon* was written by a noblewoman in the Japanese Empress's retinue over a millennium ago, in the Heian era. A compendium of wildly original lists, pointed opinions, and observations of social mores and court intrigues, its descriptions of

JAPANESE THINGS I LOVE

- Pocky
- Sei Shônagon
- Lists of Japanese things
- Old wagashi tools
- Daiso stores
- The scent of a fresh yuzu
- Hamachi sashimi
- Okinawan food
- Overcomplicated origami models
- Pretz

a time far distant are surprisingly immediate. Reading it would calm my mind, Sei Shônagon's certain, unabashed tone imposing a sense of order on my frazzled nerves.

POCKY FAR TOO GOOD TO HAVE BEEN LIMITED EDITION, I MEAN COME ON GLICO, SERIOUSLY

- Brazilian Pudding Pocky
- Crispy Pizza Pretz
- Curry Pretz
- Five Black Pocky with black pine nut, black soybean, black sugar, black sesame seeds and unpolished black rice
- Hosogiri Extra Thin Salt Caramel Pretz

Japanese popular culture still echoes Sei Shônagon's devotion to the minutiae of both old traditions and the newest nextest things. As a fusion of classic European pretzels with modern snack tech, how could Pocky not have succeeded? In 1962, Japanese confectionery firm Glico launched Pretz, a crunchy plain pretzel stick, followed four years later by Pocky Chocolate, the same stick dipped in a chocolatey coating. Its popularity expanded exponentially, eventually leading to massive diversification into regional, seasonal and global Pretz and Pocky flavours in Thailand, France, China, Canada and elsewhere.

A TAXONOMY OF POCKY AND PRETZ

- Decorer: with elaborate icing
- Double Pretz: laterally bi-flavoured stick
- Flat Style: flat sticks
- G: extra-hard and crunchy sticks
- Giant: foot-long sticks, like grissini
- Hosogiri: extra-thin sticks
- Meets Wine: formulated to go with wine
- Midi: short, stubby sticks
- Mousse: with extra-thick, fluffy icing
- Otona: flaky sticks with a layered internal structure
- Reverso: icing on the inside of a hollow stick
- Sauce: comes with tiny sachets of sauce to squeeze on top
- Tsubu-Tsubu: dipped in icing that has bits of things in it

It began innocently enough. Someone—it could've been me—brought a few boxes of Pocky to a music group rehearsal. We tore into them. At the next rehearsal, someone else brought more. It escalated. We became a gang of Pocky fanatics. Our ongoing mission: to taste as many kinds as are out there. At the time of writing, we have tasted a total of 191 different flavours.

RULES OF THE POCKY GANG

- All Pocky must be sampled
- Only that which is made by Glico shall qualify as Pocky
- The family of Pocky shall include all varieties of iced Pocky, un-iced Pretz, and giant incarnations thereof, produced in Japan or by Glico licensees outside Japan
- If any member should see a new, previously unsampled flavour of Pocky anywhere, they are bound by duty, honour and assorted threats to purchase it for subsequent tasting, budget constraints notwithstanding
- Particularly well-received Pocky varieties may of course be purchased more than once
- Pocky-like non-Glico items may also be purchased for subsequent tasting, with the full recognition that they may be of dubious legitimacy or scandalous derivativeness, and thus open to receiving disdain or outright rejection
- Pocky opened for sampling shall be passed around in an orderly and properly respectful manner, insofar as that is possible

We are not done. There will always be more.

UNATTAINED POCKY WHICH HAUNT MY DREAMS

- Sendai Grilled Beef Tongue Pretz
- Canadian Maple Syrup Pocky
- Kyushu Mikan Giant Pocky
- Kinki Uji Matcha Komimashita Pocky
- Shizuoka Unagi Giant Pretz
- Hawaiian Kona Coffee Pretz

In 1999, Glico proclaimed 11 November to be Pocky and Pretz Day, an occasion officially ratified by the Japan Anniversary Association. Its point: to buy and eat lots of Pocky.

UNNERVING THINGS

- Abalone Pretz
- Sending Pocky to a friend in Australia who then reports that each box was opened and resealed with tape by customs
- Nozawana Pickled Turnip Greens Pretz
- Decorer Pocky which has been improperly stored and thus has melted together into a slablike mess
- The price of imported Giant Pocky
- Pejoy Reverso Red Wine Chocolate
- Opening a box of Pretz to find that they are all broken.

Every day is Pocky Day in my heart.

MAKES 80 TO 100 MOCKY

INGREDIENTS

60 g	unsalted butter
125 g	cake flour
45 g	icing sugar
1	egg white
½ tsp	vanilla extract
¼ tsp	ammonium bicarbonate (page 16)
¼ tsp	fine salt
2 tsp	cool water
250 g	finely chopped chocolate, for coating

EQUIPMENT

- baking sheets lined with baking paper
- a piping bag fitted with a 3 mm plain round piping tip (such as a Wilton #6)

POINTERS

- The finer and lighter the cake flour, the more delicate (and fragile) the Mocky.
- You can add or substitute other extracts than vanilla—almond, citrus, coffee, coconut, et al.
- Don't feel you have to pipe perfectly straight lines. Slightly wonky shapes are more artisanal, *ne?*
- These never last more than two days in my house, so I'm sorry, I don't know how long they will ultimately keep.

MOCKY

Buttery, crunchy and very easy to make. I suspect most of you are wondering, given how easy it is to buy actual Pocky from physical and online shops, why you would even bother replicating it yourself? To which I reply, *because you can.*

METHOD

1 Preheat oven to 185°C. Place a shelf in the middle position.

2 Melt the butter slowly in a small pot, without letting it sizzle. Let it cool completely.

3 Sift cake flour and icing sugar together into a bowl, and whisk well to mix.

4 Add egg white and vanilla to the cooled butter and whisk until smooth. Dissolve the ammonium bicarbonate and salt in the cool water, then whisk the solution into the butter mixture. Add sifted dry ingredients to butter mixture, and stir with the whisk to make a smooth, thick, even paste.

5 Scrape the paste into the piping bag, and twist the open end to seal it. Pipe 12cm lengths of paste onto the paper-lined sheet, spacing them about 5mm apart.

6 Bake Mocky until golden brown, about 7 to 8 minutes—for the most even results, bake one sheet at a time, while you pipe the remaining Mocky. Watch them like a hawk, as they can turn from golden to burnt in a shockingly short time.

7 Transfer baking sheets to racks. Let Mocky cool completely, then transfer them to an airtight container or resealable bag. They start to soften if exposed to humid air. Keep the paper-lined baking sheets on hand.

8 Place chocolate in a heatproof bowl. Set bowl in a frying pan filled with 2 cm of barely simmering water. Stir occasionally until chocolate is almost completely melted, but some unmelted bits are still visible. Take the bowl out of the pan and stir until the chocolate is smooth, being careful not to get any water drops in it. Pour the chocolate into a clean, dry, tall and narrow vessel, such as a cup or jar. (If it is heatproof, you can pop it back into the hot water momentarily if the chocolate cools and thickens before you are done.)

9 Dip each Mocky in the chocolate, using a small spoon to help even out the coating, then place it back on the paper-lined baking sheet. Sprinkle with whatever add-ons you fancy. Continue until all the Mocky are coated. Chill the baking sheets until the chocolate is set, about 15 minutes. Carefully transfer Mocky to an airtight container, cover and store in the fridge or freezer.

DIPS AND ADD-ONS

Sure, you could go the expected route and use nuts, crushed cookies and such...but Glico has been there before you. Try these combinations instead.

- **Any chocolate + fancy salt**
  Gourmet salts will make the most visual impact on white chocolate, although any kind of chocolate benefits from the sweet-salty contrast
- **White chocolate + Japanese aonori seaweed**
  White chocolate has flavour affinities with seafood items, including these fine seaweed flakes sold in small shakers at Japanese supermarkets
- **White chocolate + poppy seeds**
- **White chocolate + furikake**
  Japanese furikake is a granulated condiment meant for sprinkling on rice, available in many flavours—try wasabi or curry furikake, whose sweet-salty-pungent flavour profiles go surprisingly well with white chocolate
- **White or dark chocolate + gochugaru**
  Gochugaru are slightly coarse chilli flakes used in Korean cooking and kimchi making, sold at Korean supermarts: the medium-hot and sweet kind brilliantly complements dark chocolate
- **Milk or dark chocolate + tenkasu**
  Tenkasu are the batter droplets which stray from tempura items as they deep-fry—small, crunchy blobs which are skimmed off and saved for garnishing noodles and other dishes; Japanese supermarkets sell them in small bags
- **White or milk chocolate + lightly toasted sesame seeds**
- **Milk chocolate + crushed vegetable chips**
  Milk chocolate pairs well with vegetal sweetness, such as those in carrot, beet, parsnip or pumpkin chips
- **Milk or dark chocolate + crushed salted potato chips**
  Warning: HIGHLY ADDICTIVE
- **Milk or dark chocolate + finely minced candied peel**
- **Dark chocolate + medium-coarse freshly ground black pepper**

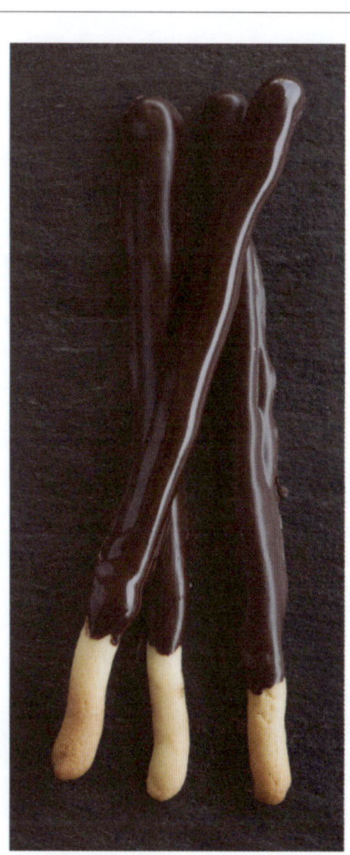

Top row, far left to right: *white choc + aonori; milk choc + beet chips; milk choc + tenkasu; milk choc + carrot chips; dark choc + gochugaru; white choc + gochugaru; Gandalf staff Mocky; white choc + soy sauce salt crystals; white choc + blueberry salt.*

Bottom row, far left to right: *dark choc + candied peel; white choc + poppy seeds; white choc + Hawaiian red salt; milk choc + parsnip chips; white choc + curry furikake; white choc + white sesame seeds; milk choc + potato chips; white choc + Hawaiian volcanic salt; milk choc + mixed sesame seeds.*

STEEP PALM & CARRY ON

Toddy, fermented sap tapped from the large flowers of various palm tree species, is responsible for the signature fragrances of many justly famed Asian cakes and breads: Filipino rice bibingka from Mandaue in Cebu, Kerala's kallappam pancakes, Goan pao loaves. Once, a colleague of mine, fresh off her flight from Indonesia, brought a kue bika ambon (page 91) from Medan to our office. When we opened the box, toddy sweetness rose up in scented waves.

Toddy tappers cut into the spikes of the palm flower, triggering a flow of thin sap which they then collect. Ambient yeasts and bacteria kick off fermentation within several minutes of the sap's exposure to the air, and over a period of hours transform the sweet, sticky liquid into a mildly alcoholic and effervescent tipple. Left to age properly, the

Top: *vintage brass mould, traditionally used for kue bluder.* **Bottom:** *Thai palm flower sap.* **Opposite:** *kue bluder.*

toddy eventually becomes vinegar—Goa and the Philippines are known for their aromatic, dulcet palm sap vinegars.

Before commercial dried yeast was sold at supermarkets, toddy was used to leaven doughs and batters in many communities all over the world. It still is in many places, but the toddy industry as a whole is dwindling, owing to uncertain demand, physically arduous labour, low profit margins, and sometimes a bad rep as cheap booze that causes social unruliness.

Its scarcity is a shame, because toddy does give a distinct lilt to what it leavens, in the same way that wild yeasts enliven lambic beers.

You can conjure up some of toddy's magic with a yeast starter made from either coconut water, the thin, slightly cloudy liquid inside a young coconut, or pasteurised versions of toddy's original substrate, coconut flower sap. Coconut water is easier to find, but be sure to get it from a fresh coconut, or choose canned versions free of additives and added sugar. Coconut flower sap is sweeter than coconut water, with an aromatic sweet corn note. Look for bottled pasteurised sap at Thai supermarkets. It may be variously and confusingly labelled 'coconut sheath juice' or 'palm juice', but labels should depict palm leaves and feathery fronds, as in the photo at left.

KUE BLUDER

SERVES 12 TO 18

INGREDIENTS

Sponge

310 g	plain flour
40 g	bread flour
1¾ tsp	osmotolerant instant yeast (page 15)
400 g	coconut water or coconut flower sap

Butter mixture

190 g	salted butter, melted and warm
1 tbsp	water
½ tsp	fine salt

Egg mixture

6	egg yolks
2	whole eggs
200 g	sugar
150 g	full cream sweetened condensed milk

EQUIPMENT

- a stand mixer fitted with the whisk beater
- a 3-litre capacity bundt pan or one-piece ring mould, sprayed with oil-and-flour baking spray, or greased and floured

POINTERS

- You can add some vanilla extract, brandy or ground mixed spice to the butter mixture in step 2, if you like.
- Some recipes incorporate dried fruit, candied peel or nuts. Dust them lightly with flour and fold them in before pouring the batter into the pan. Personally, I prefer the uninterrupted fluffiness of a plain bluder.

My rendition of a classic Indonesian kue, which has a light but rich texture, somewhere between a cake and a bread. If it reminds you of German or Alsatian kugelhopf, it should: the recipe originally comes from the Netherlands, one of the extended European family of yeasted ring cakes. Similar desserts are enjoyed by communities with Dutch colonial links, for example, Malacca's Eurasians and Sri Lanka's Dutch Burghers, who respectively call them kueh blueder and breudher.

All four countries—Holland, Indonesia, Malaysia and Sri Lanka—bake it in distinctly shaped ring moulds with straight or swirling ridges. Colloquially called 'tulband', or turban, in Dutch, modern versions of this mould are easy to find in Europe, but aren't often as elegant as antique iron or brass bluder pans, which are even rarer these days than decent toddy.

Kue bluder was traditionally leavened by toddy or other yeast sources such as tape singkong, fermented steamed cassava. Most old formulas start by making a bread dough and then enriching it with butter and eggs. I take a different tack with a yeast sponge, which yields a softer final texture.

METHOD

1 Make the sponge. Whisk plain flour, bread flour and yeast together in a bowl, then whisk in coconut water. It doesn't need to be perfectly smooth, but there should be no large pockets of dry flour. Cover and let stand for 30 to 40 minutes at room temperature, until risen to nearly twice its original volume.

2 Combine all butter mixture ingredients in a bowl and stir to dissolve salt. Set aside, covered to keep it slightly warm.

3 Combine all egg mixture ingredients in a mixing bowl. Whisk on medium speed for a full 5 to 6 minutes, until the foam is very thick and pale—when it is lifted out of the bowl, the whisk should trail a ribbon that stays on the surface for a second or two before disappearing.

4 Without deflating it first, scrape the sponge into the mixing bowl. Mix on lowest speed for 10 seconds, then scrape down the bowl sides and mix for another 10 seconds. The sponge should be almost fully incorporated.

5 While beating constantly on the lowest speed, add butter mixture to the bowl in 4 or 5 additions, mixing for about 10 seconds between each one. The batter should not deflate too much.

6 Give the batter a final stir by hand, with a large spatula, scraping the bowl sides to make sure it is evenly blended. Pour it into the prepared pan—it will be almost full. Let the pan stand at room temperature for about 40 to 50 minutes, until the batter has visibly risen just a tad. Bubbles will rise to the top—this is normal.

7 Preheat the oven to 180°C. Place a shelf in the middle position.

8 Bake kue on the middle shelf for about 45 minutes, until well browned. Small cracks may appear on top during the baking—this is

normal. It is done when it just starts to deflate, and an inserted cake tester emerges clean.

9 Let pan cool on a rack for no more than 10 minutes, then turn the kue bluder out onto a tray or plate, and let it finish cooling. It will shrink a bit as it cools, but its browned crust will help it maintain its shape. It is most wonderful served fresh and slightly warm. Its texture will firm up slightly and become more like pound cake as it reaches room temperature. Best eaten within 3 days—keep leftovers covered and chilled.

BITTERSWEET CHOCOLATE TODDY BREAD

One of my favourite breads is pandoro, a lofty Italian Christmas sweet bread. The best brands contain plenty of butter, eggs, natural yeast and real vanilla. I typically buy two or three pandoros and eke them out over a few weeks, shred by golden shred. It was while I was nursing one thusly that I noticed how much its beguiling aroma reminded me of toddy-leavened kueh. I also had lots of post-Christmas chocolate lying around. Lightbulb moment.

MAKES 2 BREADS, EACH SERVING 4 TO 6

INGREDIENTS

Custard

240 g	coconut flower sap or coconut water
40 g	cocoa powder, sifted
2	egg yolks

Sponge

50 g	coconut flower sap or coconut water
30 g	bread flour
1 tsp	osmotolerant or regular instant yeast (page 15)

Dough

2	egg whites
420 g	bread flour
10 g	potato starch
½ tsp	osmotolerant or regular instant yeast
¾ tsp	salt
1 tbsp	water
90 g	icing sugar
70 g	unsalted butter, cut into small cubes and softened
220 g	dark chocolate, chopped into small chunks
	oil, for greasing

EQUIPMENT

- a stand mixer fitted with the dough hook
- two 1.25-litre capacity pans (see pointers), sprayed with oil-and-flour baking spray, or greased and floured

METHOD

1 Combine custard ingredients in a small pot and whisk until smooth. Set over low heat and stir with a whisk, scraping the bottom and sides of the pot, until thickened to a pouring custard consistency, about 6 to 8 minutes. Let cool completely.

2 Combine sponge ingredients in a small bowl, stir to mix well, and set aside for 20 minutes. It will become bubbly as the yeast awakens.

3 Make up the dough. Combine custard, sponge, egg whites, bread flour, potato starch and yeast in a mixing bowl. Stir with a spatula to make a shaggy dough. Cover and let rest at cool room temperature for 20 minutes.

4 Dissolve the salt in the water and add to the dough. Knead dough on medium-low speed for 1 minute, then let it rest for 5 minutes. Repeat the kneading and resting twice more. The dough should become less sticky and more coherent.

5 Add icing sugar to the dough and knead on low speed until incorporated. Add the butter and knead on medium speed until the dough absorbs it and starts to pull away from the bowl sides again (it will not clean them completely), which should take about 2 minutes. The dough should now be smooth and very elastic. Cover the bowl with greased plastic wrap and let the dough stand at cool room temperature until it has risen to just over double its original volume, about 60 to 80 minutes.

6 On a lightly oiled work surface, turn out and gently deflate the dough. Divide it in half. Shape each portion into a ball. Let them relax for 10 minutes. Get your pans ready.

7 On the oiled surface, with oiled hands, press one dough portion out into a square roughly 25 cm wide, gently deflating any bubbles. Sprinkle with half the chocolate chunks and press them in. Fold the left-hand third of the dough over the middle third, then fold the right-hand third over that. Roll the resulting strip of dough up into a tight ball, and pinch all the seams well to seal. Place ball in a pan. Repeat with remaining dough, chocolate and pan. Let breads rise until doubled in size, about 35 to 45 minutes.

8 Preheat oven to 180°C. Place a shelf in a low position so that the pans will occupy the middle third of the oven.

9 Bake breads for about 30 minutes, until they are well-risen and sound hollow when tapped with a fingertip.

10 Let breads cool in their pans for 20 minutes, then unmould them onto racks and let them finish cooling. Serve breads warm, while the chocolate bits are still soft, to be torn into pieces and crammed into waiting mouths.

POINTERS

- For the best results, use a strong bread flour with a protein content of around 14 to 15 per cent.
- I use pandoro and pannettone moulds for tall and striking breads. Regular loaf pans also work well, in which case shape the dough into a log instead of a ball. Alternatively, shape the dough into a single large log, and fit it into a 2.5-litre capacity large bundt or ring pan, pinching the ends to seal.
- Use whatever dark chocolate you like, as long as it has at least 60 per cent cacao solids.
- This bread is great eaten just as it is, so you can appreciate its subtle cocoa notes and light, moist texture. It also goes well with salted butter—naturally—or cream cheese, fresh young goat cheese and berry preserves.

PURPLE REIGN

Purple is a useful colour for writers hunting metaphors, having richly accrued connotations from history and legend. It signifies everything from royalty to privilege, divinity to deviance, pretension to penitence, psychedelia to minor bruising.

It also often connotes good things to eat. I've never met a purple grain I didn't come to like. Various types are cooked across Asia, from Java to Chettinad. I grew up with bubur pulut hitam, a dessert porridge of black sticky rice, whose grains' seemingly charcoal colour is actually an intense amethyst.

As a kid, I liked its odd-looking inkiness, only later growing to love its chalky scent, like linens in old wooden drawers, and its mineral-nuanced flavour. Perhaps it's just a case of conditioned synaesthesia, but pulut hitam *tastes* purple

to me: emperor's-robe purple, Mel-Tormé-voice purple, gathering-storm purple, the underground purple of geode crystals. See, it even makes me write purple-y.

I've eaten an Italian black rice whose full flavour, poised perfectly between savoury and sweet, needed no seasoning. In Luang Prabang, I wolfed down a mix of purple and white sticky rice, a daily staple there, which stuck tenaciously to my ribs—half a bowl filled me up completely. In Manila, I sank into suman, dumplings made from violet pirurutong rice, soaked in coconut milk, folded up in banana leaves and slow-cooked until as soft as a sigh.

The following recipes call for black sticky rice flour, known as tepung pulut hitam in Malay and ketan pulut hitam in Bahasa Indonesia. Look for it at baking supply shops, Indonesian grocery stores or online.

Alternatively, if you have a high-wattage blender that can cope with dry grain, make your own flour from the whole grains. First, freeze the raw rice until it is very cold—this helps to reduce friction-generated heat from the blending. Blend it in five-second bursts until it is reduced to a fine powder. Sift the flour. If there are very coarse bits left in the sieve, return them to the blender for a second round of pulverising, then sift again. Repeat as necessary, but stop before the flour gets too warm. Store the flour in a resealable bag within an airtight container, in the fridge or freezer, where it will keep for 3 to 4 months.

Black sticky rice flour adds heft and elasticity to the crumb textures of cakes and breads, and must be mixed with wheat flour if a light final texture is desired—its flavour and colour are both assertive enough to come through nonetheless.

Top to bottom: *Laotian purple rice; pulut hitam grains and flour; Filipino purple rice.*

BLACK VELVET CUPCAKES

Indonesian cuisine has lots of recipes for black sticky rice cakes, many of them steamed—the sauna heat helps to hydrate the black rice and release its flavour. But baking works well too, if you initially soak the black sticky rice flour in some of the liquid, as here. These easy cupcakes are incredibly moist, almost fudgy, and habit-forming.

MAKES 10 CUPCAKES

INGREDIENTS

150 g	coconut milk
50 g	water
125 g	black sticky rice flour
¾ tsp	salt
125 g	plain flour
2 tsp	baking powder
2	eggs
140 g	sugar
1 tbsp	honey
100 g	unsalted butter, melted
20 g	cold-pressed coconut oil, or sunflower oil

EQUIPMENT

- 10 cupcake or muffin moulds, lined with paper cases

METHOD

1 Combine coconut milk, water, black sticky rice flour and salt in a large bowl and whisk well to mix. Cover and let stand at room temperature for 20 minutes.

2 Preheat oven to 185°C.

3 Sift plain flour and baking powder into a bowl and whisk very well to mix. Set aside.

4 Add eggs, sugar, honey, melted butter and oil to coconut milk mixture and whisk vigorously for 1 minute, scraping the sides and bottom of the bowl. Add plain flour mixture to bowl and whisk just until batter is smooth, about 8 seconds. Do not over-beat, or cupcakes will have large tunnels.

5 Divide batter between cupcake moulds. Bake cupcakes for 18 to 21 minutes, or until well risen and a tester inserted in the centre of a cupcake comes out damp but clean.

6 Transfer cupcakes to a rack to cool. Serve slightly warm or at room temperature.

POINTERS

- Use medium-thick coconut milk, about the same thickness as evaporated milk.
- Keep leftovers in an airtight container in the fridge, and let them warm up to room temperature—or steam or microwave them briefly—before serving. They are best eaten within 2 days of baking.
- The delicacy and fragrance of cold-pressed coconut oil works brilliantly here, though it is not absolutely essential.
- I like to eat these unadorned, so that the flavour of the black rice takes centre stage. That said, they do go extremely well with coconut ice cream or sorbet, warm salted coconut milk or (best of all) chilled fresh durian.

INTELLIGENT BLACK RICE CAKE

SERVES 10 TO 15

INGREDIENTS

120 g	unsalted butter
75 g	black sticky rice flour
40 g	plain flour, plus additional for dusting
275 g	coconut milk, at room temperature
200 g	warm water
½ tsp	salt
5	egg yolks
135 g	caster sugar
40 g	condensed milk
5	egg whites
½ tsp	cream of tartar
	oil, for greasing

EQUIPMENT

- a deep 23 cm round cake pan, preferably with a removable base
- heavy-duty foil
- a cake mixer fitted with the whisk beater

POINTERS

- Use medium-thick coconut milk (see previous page).
- The topmost cake layer has a slight insulating effect on the custard beneath it, which won't fully set if you under-bake it. If in doubt as to the cake's done-ness, bake it a few minutes longer—the batter is sufficiently moist that it is unlikely to dry out.
- This cake slices much more neatly, and the separation between the layers is more apparent, after it has been chilled.
- Slight differences in flour protein content and egg size will change the relative thicknesses of the three layers. Every cake's IQ is different.

Like pandas and mahogany trees, self-separating desserts belong to a genus with few but significant members. Notable ones are self-saucing puddings, lemon honeycomb jellies, and coconut and gula melaka agar-agar.

I humbly submit my addition to the canon. Don't worry, it won't ask to see your leader—this recipe is a riff on a Romanian dessert called prăjitură deşteaptă, literally translated as 'smart cake'. It merits its name because, all by itself, without any Béla Károlyi coaching, it does the splits as it bakes, into three different layers. Its bottom layer is dense and toothsome, exactly like many kinds of Peranakan and Malay kueh; its middle layer is a smooth, light custard; and crowning the whole is an airy chiffon cake.

The miracle stems from a high liquid content: whipped egg whites folded into the watery batter naturally rise to the top, while the starch fraction sinks to the bottom. The heavy nature and slow hydration rate of black rice flour enhance the separation. The flavours of black rice and coconut milk also suit the tri-layered structure to a tee—you might think this was a steamed Asian kueh if you didn't know its Romanian roots.

METHOD

1 Line the pan with heavy-duty foil, creasing and pleating it to lie neat and flat against the tin sides. Grease and flour the base and sides of the foil liner.

2 Preheat oven to 160°C, on conventional top and bottom heat—*do not use fan assistance*. Place a shelf in the middle position, and a heavy baking sheet on the shelf.

3 Melt the unsalted butter and keep it slightly warm.

4 Sift the black sticky rice flour and plain flour into a bowl. Whisk well to blend. Set aside.

5 Whisk coconut milk, warm water and salt together until blended. Set aside.

6 Combine egg yolks, sugar and condensed milk in a mixing bowl. Beat on medium speed until very thick and fluffy, and the whisk trails a thick ribbon when it is lifted out of the bowl. This should take 4 to 5 minutes.

7 Pour melted butter into bowl and beat on high speed until completely incorporated. Add flour mixture and beat on medium-low speed until it is blended in. Scrape down the bowl sides. Slowly add coconut milk mixture, beating constantly on low speed, until smooth—the batter will rapidly thin out. Set it aside momentarily.

8 In a clean, grease-free bowl, beat egg whites with cream of tartar just until stiff peaks form. Do not over-beat—the foam should still be slightly shiny, not matte and dry-looking.

9 With a large spatula, fold the egg whites into the batter in two additions. They are tricky to combine because of their radically different consistencies, and it will

look terrible at first, but just keep folding gently, scraping the bowl's sides and bottom and drawing the spatula up through the batter, until there are no large lumps or streaks of egg white. The batter will finally look billowy and loose, like melted cheap ice cream.

10 Pour batter into prepared pan. Place on the baking sheet and bake for 65 to 70 minutes. The cake will dome and brown—don't worry about cracks, they will close up as the cake cools and settles. It is done when a skewer inserted into the middle of the cake comes out damp but clean, with no stringy, eggy stuff clinging to it.

11 Transfer cake tin to a rack. The cake will shrink and flatten as it cools—if it threatens to tear away messily from the pan's rim, run a knife around its edge to free it so it can contract evenly. Once it has completely cooled, cover pan with plastic wrap and chill it until cold, at least 2 hours. Unmould cake by pushing the pan base (or lifting the foil) out of the pan. Peel away foil from the cake's sides. To serve, slice with a sharp knife.

EGG WAFERS
RM2.00
SESAME CRACKER
RM1.80
RICE BISCUITS
RM3.80
GREEN PEAS BIS
RM3.80
RM 2.50

PACKET WATCH

When I moved to England in my teens, one of the most comically jarring cultural dislocations was between what the British meant by 'biscuit' versus what the word meant in Singapore.

The biscuits I grew up with were distant descendants of Anglo originals, filtered through Asian taste preferences and hazy ingredient substitutions. Powdery coconut-cassava shards which rained dander everywhere and tasted like plaster of Paris; supposedly cheese-flavoured batons, crunchy and oddly addictive despite a merely tangential likeness to cheese; chewy piglet-shaped treats in

plastic baskets, occupying an agreeable zone between pastry, cake and biscuit. Some I actively loathed. Kueh koya, gritty nuggets of ground mung beans, could crack a tooth, a jaw, a skull if bitten into recklessly, and tasted to me of centenarian tortoises, full of minerals and accumulated disgruntlement.

Some had an authentically English connection, like the Horlicks biscuits doled out stingily at school sports events. Marie biscuits I inhaled in massive quantities, but paid zero actual attention to; like kids everywhere, I picked the royal icing bullets off iced gems and ignored the biscuit part.

We seldom ate Jacob's cream crackers with cheese in the British manner, but more often crushed them to coat things destined for deep-frying, or slathered them with butter and drifts of white sugar—a treat which is to a hyperactive child as a propane tank is to an arsonist.

Then England changed my world with the rustle of a Hobnobs wrapper. Jaffa Cakes undid all my self-restraint. Rich Tea biscuits made me forget Marie forever. Jammie Dodgers turned out to be the Narnian versions of the cardboard-and-creosote 'jam'-centred biscuits sold at old Chinese provision shops. Sainsbury's chocolate chip digestives fuelled study binges in my uni days.

But the ones which really won my heart were custard creams. These were custard in a biscuit in a wholly more exalted, rapturous way than Chicken-In-A-Biskit was ever anything like chicken in a biscuit. I would open a pack in front of the TV, lose myself in Christmas Day specials, then suddenly come to my senses hours later, surrounded by crumbs and shreds of plastic. Good times.

Opposite, clockwise from top left:
Chinese spiral biscuits; goldfish crackers; wafer biscuits filled with durian cream; iced gems and cream crackers; wafer envelopes folded around peanut powder; 'ngau kok pang', 'buffalo horn' biscuits from Ipoh, filled with peanut powder.

MAKES 35 TO 40 SANDWICH BISCUITS

INGREDIENTS

Dough

220 g	plain flour
45 g	custard powder
55 g	icing sugar
160 g	cold unsalted butter, cubed
1	small egg yolk
1 tsp	vanilla extract
1 tsp	water
⅛ tsp	salt

Filling

150 g	milk
100 g	caster sugar
20 g	custard powder
tiny pinch	salt
170 g	unsalted butter, cubed and softened until just barely spreadable
1 tsp	vanilla bean paste or vanilla extract

EQUIPMENT

- a cake mixer fitted with the paddle attachment
- baking sheets lined with baking paper

CUSTARD CREAMS

You can always make plain unstamped cookies, but mottoes are half the fun.

METHOD

1 Make the dough. Sift plain flour, custard powder and icing sugar into a mixing bowl. Mix on medium-low speed with the paddle attachment for 45 seconds to blend. Add butter and continue mixing until it has dispersed and the mixture resembles fine sand.

2 Beat egg yolk, vanilla, water and salt together until salt dissolves. Drizzle it over the flour-butter mixture, mixing on lowest speed just until the dough coheres into a ball. Knead it with your hand for 5 to 8 seconds, just to even it out. Shape it into a flat disc, wrap in plastic wrap and chill it for at least 1 hour, until cold but malleable.

3 Sandwich the dough between sheets of baking paper and roll it out until it is about 4 mm thick. Chill the rolled-out dough, in its paper sandwich, for 1 hour and up to 24 hours.

4 Peel off top paper layer. Cut dough into square, oblong or round biscuits about 4 cm across. Space them out on the paper-lined baking sheets, about 1.5 cm apart—they will not spread much. Decorate with a letterpress stamp, if desired. Cover the biscuits with plastic wrap and chill them on their sheets for at least 30 minutes, until cold and firm.

5 Preheat oven to 180°C. Place a shelf in the middle position.

6 Bake the biscuits one sheet at a time for 10 to 12 minutes, until light golden brown. Transfer baking sheet to a rack to cool. Only move the biscuits to an airtight container once they are completely cool, as they are fragile while warm.

7 Make the filling. Combine milk, caster sugar, custard powder and salt in a small pot, whisk well to blend and set over low heat. Cook, whisking constantly, until very gloopy and sticky, resembling lemon curd, and a couple of large bubbles bloop to the surface. Scrape into a fine mesh strainer set over a bowl and press it through. Let cool to room temperature.

8 Transfer custard paste to a mixing bowl. Start beating with the paddle attachment on medium-high speed, and add butter a tablespoon at a time every 4 seconds, until it has all been incorporated and filling is light, smooth and homogenous. Beat in vanilla. Transfer filling to an airtight container and chill until firmed up slightly.

9 Spoon or pipe a little filling onto half the biscuits, then top with the remaining biscuits, pressing lightly so they adhere. Keep chilled in an airtight container until serving time.

POINTERS

- Dusting cookie cutters and stamps with rice flour helps prevent sticking. I stamp designs on all the biscuits, then use the uglier ones as the bases.
- Many custard cream recipes whip up a filling from butter, sugar and raw custard powder. I don't care for the latter's chalkiness, so my filling is a modified eggless buttercream. It is fiddly to make in smaller quantities, so you will have some filling left over. Kept chilled in an airtight container, it will last a few days.
- The assembled custard creams will slowly soften as the biscuits absorb moisture from the filling—not necessarily a bad thing. Serve them on the day of assembly for maximum texture contrast.

MAKES 25 TO 28 BISCUITS

INGREDIENTS

Dry ingredients

110 g	plain flour
40 g	cake flour
160 g	white sugar
2 tbsp	white sesame seeds, plus additional for garnish
2½ tsp	five-spice powder
¾ tsp	finely and freshly ground pepper
½ tsp	ground cinnamon
½ tsp	ground ginger

Wet ingredients

1	egg
1½ tsp	nam yee, mashed (see pointers)
2 tsp	liquid from the nam yee jar
⅔ tsp	fine salt
1 tbsp	fried shallots in oil
1 clove	garlic, finely minced
1 tsp	ammonium bicarbonate (page 16)
50 g	lard
20 g	smooth peanut butter
	oil, for greasing

EQUIPMENT

- a blender or small food processor
- baking sheets lined with baking paper

Nam yee, tofu fermented with red yeast rice.

CHINESE FIVE-SPICE SNAPS

Virtually every old-school Chinese bakery in Singapore and Malaysia sells spiral biscuits (page 69), made of a crisp, hard plain dough vortexed together with crunchy, peppery, red-tinted dough. Dipped quickly into hot coffee or tea and then left to dissolve into raspy crumbs on my tongue, they are like crack to me. Most bakeries now import rather than make them, and so buying them is like reverse Russian roulette—good ones are rare, most are cardboardy and blah. So instead I make these snaps—with the red dough, without fake colouring and its plain dough sidekick, neither of which I liked anyway. The ingredients list probably reads like a cruel horror story if you only know Western gingersnaps—garlic! shallots! slimy red tofu! a stupid amount of pepper! ammonia, for crying out loud!—but I promise you, the sum is far, far, far more than the individual parts. These are snaps for pirates—biting, spicy, funky, savoury, a little bit nutty.

METHOD

1 Whisk all the dry ingredients together in a mixing bowl until well blended.

2 Combine all the wet ingredients except the lard and peanut butter in a blender or small food processor. Blend until smooth. Add lard and peanut butter, and blend until emulsified into a smooth, pale orange mixture.

3 Scrape the wet ingredients into dry ingredients. Stir with a spatula into a sticky dough. Lightly grease a lidded container with oil, scrape dough into it, smooth it out, and cover. Chill for at least 8 hours and up to 24 hours.

4 Preheat oven to 175°C. Place a shelf in the middle position.

5 Roll heaped teaspoonfuls of dough into small balls, about 20 g each. Dip each ball in white sesame seeds. Place them on the baking sheet, seeds upwards, spaced at least 7 cm apart, as they will spread. Flatten them slightly until they are about 1 cm thick. Alternatively, dust each ball with cornstarch, then space them out likewise and flatten them with a decorative stamp—the pattern will leave just a trace after baking, like an archaeological earthwork.

6 Bake the biscuits for 13 to 15 minutes, one sheet at a time. Keep the raw dough chilled in between shaping batches.

7 Transfer baking sheets to racks to cool. (Avert your face when you open the oven, lest you get socked by any lingering ammonia fumes.) The hot biscuits are very soft but will firm up as they cool. As soon as they reach room temperature, transfer them to an airtight container and store in the fridge. They will taste better the next day.

POINTERS

- Nam yee, tofu fermented with red yeast rice, is sold in jars or crocks at Chinese provision shops. (See photo on facing page.) Don't be creeped out by its looks—it has a pleasant sweet, yeasty, slightly cheesy aroma. As a substitute, use a good yellow or white miso, and reduce the salt to ½ teaspoon.
- Chinese shops and supermarkets also stock crispy-fried shallots in oil. Dry fried shallots are fine to substitute, as long as they aren't thickly coated with flour. Alternatively, substitute one small raw purple shallot, finely minced.
- The spices must be really fresh.
- Ammonium bicarbonate is necessary for these biscuits to turn out airy and crunchy without also being over-baked. You can substitute ½ teaspoon double-acting baking powder plus ⅓ teaspoon bicarbonate of soda, but the snaps won't be quite as light, and you may need to increase the baking time slightly.
- These snaps bake better in a fan-assisted oven—the moving air makes them puff and dry out more evenly, and disperses the ammonia fumes from the activated leavening.

MAKES ABOUT 15 BISCUITS

INGREDIENTS

Sugar-cured lard

125 g	pork fat, cut into fingernail-size dice
125 g	caster sugar
2 tbsp	mei kuei lu jiu (Chinese rose rice liquor)

Toasted mung beans

150 g	skinned split mung beans

Dough

100 g	toasted mung beans
20 g	tapioca starch
70 g	icing sugar
⅓ tsp	salt
80 g	cake flour
65 g	cold unsalted butter, cut into small cubes
60 g	lard, very cold
½ tsp	almond extract
50 g	flaked almonds, lightly toasted and cooled
	rice flour, for dusting
	vegetable oil, for greasing biscuit moulds

EQUIPMENT

- a blender or food processor
- a cake mixer fitted with the paddle attachment
- a wooden biscuit mould
- baking sheets, lined with baking paper

HUNG NGAN PANG

CHINESE ALMOND BISCUITS

I have childhood memories of relatives returning from trips to Hong Kong and Macau with gaily-decorated metal tins, like lidded pails with handles. Inside were biscuits, embossed with pretty patterns and Chinese characters.

How I hated them.

If they didn't crumble when you picked them up, they shed dust all over your hands and clothes, then fragmented into shrapnel and dust in your mouth, spreading the taste of not-quite-fresh lard all over your palate. Worst of all, buried in the bitter-almondy grit were slippery bits of candied pork fat. Why would people eat these?

Fast forward a few decades. Commercial hung ngan pang are now mostly lard-free, and also flavour-free. My adult palate now digs pork fat and subtle bitterness, and I would gladly trade the depressing pucks of today for the hung ngan pang of yesteryear. But the real things are now scarce, and few people are mad enough to make them at home.

I am, of course. But not totally—traditional hung ngan pang are made by compacting a barely moistened, powdery almond and mung bean mixture into moulds, then baking the turned-out biscuits at a low temperature until they harden. This is not unlike how particleboard is made. My recipe instead yields a slightly puffed, shortbread-like result, lighter and crunchier. These call for serious commitment, but are rich, nutty, nuanced and addictive.

In the final analysis, however weird these may seem, they are not and never will be as bizarre as Twiglets.

Traditional hung ngan pang in Macau.

METHOD

1 *Make the sugar-cured lard a week beforehand.* Combine all the ingredients in a small, clean glass jar. Stir to mix thoroughly, then cover tightly and store in the fridge for 7 to 10 days. Shake the jar every day to redistribute the sugar.

2 Cook the mung beans: rinse them well, drain, then add them to a pot of steadily simmering water and cook until tender, 12 to 15 minutes. Drain them well, and spread them out on a baking sheet lined with baking paper. Bake in a preheated oven at 150°C for 25 to 35 minutes, stirring occasionally, until the mung beans are dry and crisp. Do not over-bake them or they will become too hard. Let cool completely.

3 Weigh out 100 g of the toasted mung beans, and pulse-blend them with the tapioca starch in a blender or food processor until they are very finely pulverised. Add sugar, salt, cake flour and blanched almonds, and blend until the almonds are ground very fine. Tip the mixture into a mixing bowl. It will be warm from the friction of the blending. Cover and chill for at least 30 minutes until cool.

4 Add the butter, lard and almond extract to the dry ingredients. With the paddle attachment, mix on low speed until the fats disperse and the mixture looks like fine sand. Stir in the toasted flaked almonds. Bring the crumbly dough together with your hands, kneading it briefly to even it out and compact it. Wrap dough in plastic wrap and let it rest in the fridge for 8 hours.

5 About 20 minutes before you start shaping and baking the hung ngan pang, brush the wooden moulds lightly with vegetable oil, and let them sit—the wood will absorb the oil, aiding the clean release of the biscuits later.

6 Place sugar-cured lard in a bowl and cover with water just off the boil. Let sit for 20 seconds, then drain well and blot dry.

7 Divide dough into small balls. Their precise size depends on the size of your moulds—mine takes 30 g portions. Embed 1 or 2 pieces of lard in the centre of a ball, and pinch the dough to surround and seal them in. Dust the ball evenly with rice flour, then press it firmly into the mould. Tap the mould sharply on the countertop to release the biscuit into your hand. Place the biscuits on the paper-lined baking sheets, spacing them at least 4 cm apart. Repeat with remaining dough and lard.

8 Chill the moulded biscuits on the baking sheets for at least 30 minutes, until they are cold.

9 Preheat oven to 180°C. Place a shelf in the middle position.

10 Bake biscuits one sheet at a time for 12 to 14 minutes, until golden. Transfer baking sheet to a rack to cool. Once biscuits are cool, store in an airtight container in the fridge or freezer.

POINTERS

- Ready-made roasted mung bean flour almost always tastes stale, gritty and dusty. Toasting your own mung beans (pictured below) results in far better colour and flavour.

- If you don't eat lard, omit the candied lard, and substitute cold-pressed coconut oil for the lard in the dough—measure it out and freeze it until solid before use. The biscuits will still be very good.
- Look for wood or plastic biscuit moulds in Chinese cookware shops. As long as the hollows are not more than 1 cm deep and not more than 6 cm wide, they are fine for hung ngan pang.

2.

RELATIVELY SPEAKING

The most exciting, energising feeling in the experience of eating is the "Oh I've never tasted this before!" instant, when one's mind and world expand to welcome a new flavour or texture. A close second, or maybe first equal, is that other feeling of "Oh I've tasted this before, but not this way!" Wise cooks know that what keeps people taking another bite, and another, is the interplay of familiarity and strangeness, tugging synapses in different directions. That's why it's so galvanising, when you're miles away from foods you know, to come across a new taste that would fit right in with them.

Historians gave the name 'the Age of Discovery' to the era of European-led globetrotting and colonial conquests. But the human drive to find and own something new, yet something familiar, didn't start then, nor did it cease afterwards. Empires have always grown, clashed and receded, and will continue to do so, though these days they send out optic cables instead of ships, and stake claims on mindshare instead of turf.

Beneath the tangled web of trade and dominion that humans have woven over the world is a tracery of culinary connections and repercussions, written in the flourish of a ladle and the sprinkle of a spice. For me, the most stirring seasoning for any dish is the story of its heritage and its kinships. This chapter celebrates those ties.

SHORT & SWEET

Shortbread cookies stuffed with dried fruit or nuts are baked across the Arabic-speaking world, and many other communities in the Middle East and Western Asia.

Muslims, Christians and Jews each have their own versions, savoured at respective festivals and special occasions. Lebanese and Armenian Christians make them for Easter, Iraqi Jews for Purim, Muslims everywhere for Eid-al-Adha. 'Maamoul', spelt in various ways, is the most common name given to these crumbly treats, which are invariably shaped with carved moulds or other means. In Singapore and Malaysia, for example, Malay kueh makmur are typically filled with ground roasted peanuts and sugar, and incised with decorative lines from serrated pincers.

The basic recipe has an ancient pedigree. Medieval cookbook manuscripts from Syria and Egypt document various kinds of small stuffed baked goods, two of which may be proto-maamoul: irnin, filled with pistachios, almonds or dates and shaped with a mould, and khushkananaj, stuffed with almonds and hand-shaped. While they both use sesame oil in the dough, as compared to the butter more common today, in all other respects they are practically identical to modern maamoul recipes.

For my recipes, I've combined untraditional fruit and nut fillings with mostly classic doughs and a touch of whimsy.

CASHEW CACAO PEPPER MAKMUR

MAKES 23 TO 28 COOKIES

INGREDIENTS

Dough

160 g	unsalted butter
¼ tsp	vanilla extract
180 g	cake flour
75 g	icing sugar, plus additional for dredging
50 g	cornstarch
¼ tsp	double-acting baking powder
⅓ tsp	fine salt

Filling

100 g	roasted salted cashew nuts
15 g	roasted cacao nibs
1¾ tsp	coarsely and freshly ground black pepper
30 g	light brown sugar
	rice flour, for dusting

EQUIPMENT

- a baking sheet lined with baking paper
- a maamoul mould (see pointers)

POINTERS

- Yield and cooking time will both vary according to mould size. Here I've used a 30 ml-capacity maamoul mould, which yielded 25 cookies that baked through in 18 minutes. Smaller cookies will bake faster.

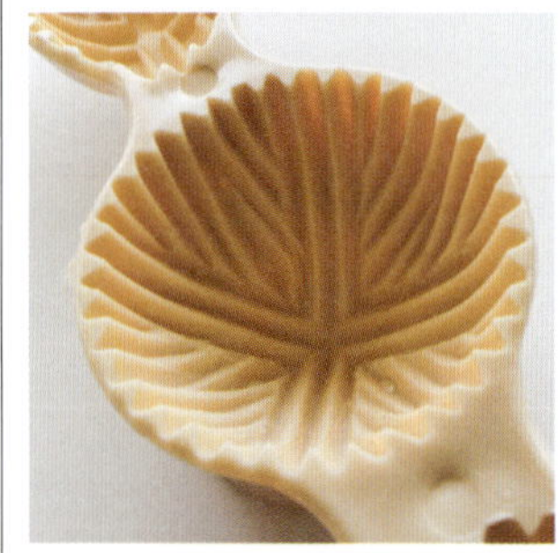

In the late 1980s, Cantonese restaurants in Singapore would always serve diners a pre-meal nibble, often without the surcharges commanded by such bouche-amusing snacks today. One of my favourites was cashew nuts, deep-fried to a teak brown and glazed with sugar, salt and black pepper. I've translated that taste memory into Malay-style kueh makmur, with the added fillip of roasted cacao nibs—dark chocolate, pepper and cashews are very natural bedfellows. The clarified butter dough is easy to work with and is meltingly crumbly.

METHOD

1 Clarify the butter. Melt it in a small pot over medium-low heat and cook it, stirring frequently, until it stops sizzling and the milk solids clump and sink to the bottom—take care not to let them scorch. Strain the butter through a fine sieve, discarding solids. Stir in the vanilla and let it cool completely.

2 Make the dough. Sift cake flour, icing sugar, cornstarch and baking powder together into a mixing bowl. Add salt and whisk well to blend. Add cooled clarified butter and mix into a claylike dough with a spatula. Wrap dough in plastic wrap and chill overnight.

3 Make the filling. Grind cashew nuts in a food processor until about the same size as the cacao nibs. It's fine—and in fact, better—if they are a bit uneven, with mixed fine and chunky bits. Transfer nuts to a bowl and stir in all remaining ingredients.

4 Preheat oven to 170°C. Place a shelf in the middle position.

5 Pinch off a walnut-sized ball of dough. Roll it between your palms to soften it up and make it malleable. Shape it into a cup, moulding it around a thumbtip, making the walls about 3 to 4 mm thick and as even as you can. Spoon a little filling into the cup, pressing it in to compact it slightly. Press the cup rim together to seal, pinching off any excess dough if necessary. Dust the resulting ball lightly with rice flour, then press it into your chosen mould—I've used a classic round maamoul mould for the photographed cookies. Tap it out onto the baking sheet. Make all makmur likewise, spacing them about 3 cm apart.

6 Bake makmur for 17 to 20 minutes, until pale gold. Do not overbake, unless you prefer them crunchy through and through. Transfer baking sheet to a rack. Let makmur stand until completely cooled and firm. Store them in an airtight container. They will keep for at least 10 days in the fridge. Dredge lightly in icing sugar before serving.

APRICOT-THYME MAAMOUL

MAKES 30 COOKIES

INGREDIENTS

Dough

130 g	unsalted butter, melted and cooled
50 g	water
30 g	sugar
½ tsp	salt
1	egg
½ tsp	almond extract
180 g	fine semolina (see pointers)
140 g	plain flour
¼ tsp	osmotolerant instant yeast (page 15)

Filling

3 tbsp	mild honey or apricot jam
1 tbsp	hot water
2 tsp	lemon juice
1 tsp	finely minced fresh thyme leaves
½ tsp	finely grated lemon zest
200 g	dried apricots (see pointers), finely chopped
	rice flour, for dusting
	icing sugar, for dredging

EQUIPMENT

- baking sheets lined with baking paper
- a maamoul mould (see pointers)

The aromas of apricot, honey, lemon and thyme harmonise as exquisitely as the Von Trapp children, wrapped in a Middle-Eastern style maamoul dough with a buttery, bready crunch. Neither dough nor filling are very sweet, so dredge generously with icing sugar to balance out the flavours.

METHOD

1 Make the dough. Whisk melted butter, water, sugar, salt, egg and almond extract together until smooth. Add semolina and stir slowly with a spatula for 1 minute. The semolina will absorb the liquid and become a sludgy paste. Whisk flour and yeast together, then add to the bowl and fold until evenly blended in. Do not overwork. Wrap dough in plastic wrap and chill for at least 3 hours.

2 Make the filling. Combine all ingredients except the apricots and stir until well-mixed, then fold in apricots. Cover tightly and chill for at least 4 hours to let the apricots soften.

3 Preheat oven to 175°C. Place a shelf in the middle position.

4 Divide the dough into 30 equal portions. Press 1 portion into a flat disc about 2 to 3 mm thick, slightly thinner at its rim. Place a scant teaspoon of filling on the disc's centre, then bring up the edges to enclose the filling. Pinch well to seal. Dust the resulting ball all over with rice flour, press it into the maamoul mould, then tap it out onto the baking sheet. Make all maamoul likewise, spacing them about 3 cm apart.

5 Bake the maamoul one sheet at a time for 19 to 22 minutes, until golden and cooked through. Place baking sheet on a rack and let the maamoul stand until completely cooled, firm and crisp. Store them in an airtight container. They will keep for at least 10 days in the fridge. Dredge with icing sugar before serving.

POINTERS

- Fine semolina, shown at right in a spoon, is faintly gritty, but finer than polenta or cornmeal. It is not the same as durum wheat flour or semolina flour for pasta.
- Use sulphured dried apricots—the orange kind. Unsulphured dark brown apricots have too strong a caramel flavour for this recipe.

- Don't make these cookies too small. I find that a yield of 30 results in a filling-to-dough ratio that has the best balance of crunch and chew in the mouth.
- I shaped these by pressing them into the very bottom of the floral agar-agar jelly mould shown opposite. Be creative—you could also use Chinese cookie or cake moulds.

BANANA MAAMOUL

Sticky sun-dried bananas have a wonderful 'banoffee' flavour and a fudgy, chewy consistency much like dates, and hence make a brilliant filling for these unconventional maamoul. Look for them in health food shops or Thai grocery stores.

MAKES 25 TO 30 COOKIES

INGREDIENTS

Dough

160 g	cake flour
75 g	icing sugar
60 g	cornstarch
¼ tsp	double-acting baking powder
⅓ tsp	fine salt
125 g	cold unsalted butter, diced
3 tbsp	chocolate rice
1	egg yolk
1½ tsp	vanilla extract or natural banana extract

Filling

200 g	sun-dried bananas
2½ tbsp	honey
1 tbsp	water
1	egg white, beaten, for glazing

EQUIPMENT

- a cake mixer fitted with the paddle attachment
- a baking sheet lined with baking paper

METHOD

1 Make the dough. Sift cake flour, icing sugar, cornstarch and baking powder together into a mixing bowl. Add salt and mix on low speed for 1 minute to blend.

2 While beating constantly on low speed, add butter to bowl. Mix until it has dispersed and mixture looks like very fine crumbs. Add chocolate rice and mix to combine.

3 Add egg yolk and vanilla to bowl and beat for several seconds on the lowest speed, until dough comes together into a ball. Knead dough briefly by hand to even it out, then wrap in plastic wrap and chill it for at least 4 hours or overnight.

4 Make the filling. Finely mince dried bananas, then stir together with honey and water in a small bowl. Cover tightly and let stand for 1 hour to let the bananas hydrate a little.

5 Preheat oven to 170°C. Place a shelf in the middle position.

6 Divide the dough into portions of 16 to 18 g each. Sandwich a portion between two sheets of plastic wrap and roll it into an oval about 6.5 cm long by 4 cm wide. Peel off top sheet of plastic wrap. Spoon about ¾ teaspoon of filling down the long axis of the oval, shaping it into a neat, skinny log. Using the bottom sheet of plastic wrap to help you, roll the dough around the filling, making a cigar shape. Pinch seam and ends to seal. Place the maamoul on a baking sheet, seam downwards, curving it like a banana. Repeat with remaining dough and filling to make all cookies. Space them about 2 cm apart on the baking sheet, as they will expand slightly.

7 Brush the maamoul lightly with beaten egg white. Bake for 16 to 18 minutes, until pale gold. Transfer baking sheet to a rack. Let maamoul cool completely before transferring them to an airtight container for storage. They will keep for at least 10 days in the fridge.

THE BINGKA EMPIRE

If you've eaten widely around Asia, you may have noticed the prevalence of different cakes and kueh called 'bingka' (or spelling variations thereof).

There are Filipino bibingkas, made from a rice or wheat batter leavened with yeast or baking powder, baked in banana-leaf cups.

In Macau, bebinca de leite is a thick-set custard of coconut milk and cornstarch. Many-layered Goan bibinca is laid down and grilled one decadent strata at a time. Southern India also has several rice cakes which are bingkas in all but name, such as Kerala's savoury-sweet kalathappam, dusky with jaggery and studded with chunks of coconut, ginger and shallots. Malay and Indonesian cuisines have many bingkas, bengkas and bikas: among the most famous are Medan's kue bika ambon, lavishly endowed with citrus fragrance and air bubbles, and Malaysian/Singaporean kueh bengka, buttery and dense with grated cassava. What the members of the extended bingka family have in common: they are invariably baked, usually stodgy from well-hydrated grain or tuber starches, and often quite rich from quantities of eggs, coconut or sugar.

Clockwise from far left, bottom: *Chris' plain bingka; cheese bingka; brownie bingka; and blueberry bingka.*

Armchair historians will have spotted that all the above cultures share historical connections with Portugal, whether through colonial occupation or trade routes. (Desserts deriving their names from 'bolo', Portuguese for 'cake', are also common across the same regions and nations.) However, 'bingka' is not a Portuguese word, and scholars seem undecided as to who coined it, or how it was so widely adopted and adapted. The closest-sounding Asian words are 'bengkak' (swollen) and 'bengkang' (curved), in both Malay and Indonesian—plausible roots, given that many bingkas rise and swell as they cook.

I have another hypothesis. The great majority of bingkas are traditionally baked in a pan or mould sandwiched between two heat sources, such as a wood or coconut-husk fire, or glowing coals (right, bottom).

A cast-iron vessel specifically designed for this cooking method, with a flat or footed base and a lipped cover, was refined and popularised by the Dutch from the 18th century onwards, hence its colloquial name, 'Dutch oven'—and as we know, many former Portuguese colonies in Asia were also vied for and influenced by the Dutch. Another trait shared by many bingkas is a spongy internal texture, quite pronounced in some recipes—bika ambon is so tunnel-riddled that it resembles a honeycomb. Honeycombs are found in beehives. 'Beehive' in Dutch is 'bijenkorf', pronounced 'bayenkorf'. Could this be the root of 'bingka'? I may be entirely mistaken, but the possibility is entertaining to entertain...and a reminder that food so often connects us all.

Left, top to bottom: *a bibingka stall; salted egg, waiting to be topped with bibingka batter.* ***Opposite, clockwise from top left:*** *Malay rice bingka; kue bika ambon; Chris' black rice bingka; classic Filipino bibingka, almost done.*

MAKES 12 MUFFIN-SIZED BINGKA

INGREDIENTS

Dough

200 g	idli rice (see pointers)
35 g	glutinous rice
240 g	boiled and cooled water
25 g	tapioca starch
155 g	sugar
115 g	coconut cream
½ tsp	salt
3	eggs
1¼ tsp	osmotolerant instant yeast (page 15)
75 g	melted butter
1¾ tsp	baking powder

EQUIPMENT

- a blender
- a standard muffin pan with 12 hollows
- banana leaves

POINTERS

- Sold in Indian grocery stores, idli rice is parboiled short grain rice favoured in South India for making rice breads and cakes such as dosas, appams and idlis. Compared to raw rice, idli rice produces a lighter, more even final texture in these and similar items, including bingka.
- Tapioca starch contributes softness, glutinous rice springiness.
- If your tap water has a high mineral or chlorine content, filter it before using it to rinse and soak the rice.
- Wipe fresh banana leaves on both sides with a damp cloth before further prep. They can keep for 2 to 3 days if wrapped loosely in newspaper and stashed in the fridge vegetable drawer.

CHRIS' BINGKA

For this recipe, I have cherry-picked and combined ingredients and techniques from across the bingka empire: Filipino bibingka's banana-leaf cradles, parboiled rice from Southern India, Singaporean kueh bengka's dose of butter, and so on.

METHOD

1 Rinse idli rice once, drain well and place in a lidded container. Rinse and drain glutinous rice likewise and combine with the idli rice. Add water to the container to cover the rice by 2 cm. Cover and refrigerate for 22 to 24 hours.

2 Drain the rice well, discarding all the soaking water. Combine rice with 120 g of the boiled and cooled water in a blender and blend until rice breaks down into a smooth slurry—when you rub some between your fingers, you should only feel a mere ghost of grittiness. This may take a few minutes depending how powerful your blender is.

3 Add remaining 120 g boiled and cooled water, tapioca starch, sugar, coconut cream, salt and eggs to the blender, and blend until smooth. Pour batter into a bowl and whisk in yeast. Cover bowl and let stand at cool room temperature for 1½ to 2 hours, until batter is a bit frothy and smells slightly yeasty.

4 Cut out circles or squares of banana leaf big enough to line your muffin pans and extend about 5 mm above their rims. Blanch the banana leaf pieces in boiling water for 30 seconds, until they are flexible. Drain them. With the darker, shinier side of the leaf facing upwards, tuck a circle or square into each pan hollow, gathering or pleating the sides to fit.

5 Preheat oven to 200°C, *using conventional top and bottom heat*—this mimics the traditional bingka cooking conditions. Place a shelf in the lowest position.

6 Whisk melted butter into batter, then sift in baking powder and whisk hard until very well combined. Pour batter into pans. It should come up to 6 or 7 mm below the rims of the banana leaves.

7 Bake for 30 to 35 minutes, until risen and browned, and a cake tester inserted into the centre of a bingka emerges damp but mostly clean. If bingka tops aren't browning enough for your liking, move the shelf to a higher position for the last 10 minutes of baking.

8 Serve bingkas warm or at room temperature. They are best eaten within 2 days of baking. Steam or microwave leftovers to reheat before serving.

STEP 4

VARIATIONS

- **Cheese bingka**
  Salty, lightly pungent cheeses are great additions. Fold a large handful of grated Gouda, Edam or cheddar into the batter, and sprinkle more to taste over the bingkas after they have baked for about 10 minutes.
- **Blueberry bingka**
  Add a few blueberries to each bingka before putting them to bake. The berries make the bingkas more moist, custardy and perishable.
- **Brownie bingka**
  For one full recipe, whisk 18 g of sifted cocoa powder, 1 tablespoon water and 2 teaspoons muscovado sugar into the melted butter until smooth, then whisk it into the batter as in step 6. The cocoa makes these slightly cake-like. Don't overbake them.
- **Black rice bingka**
  For one full recipe, substitute 40 g black sticky rice for the glutinous rice, increase the boiled and cooled water to 260 g in total, and reduce the tapioca starch to 20 g. Substantial and fragrant, these are best baked as 6 large bingkas (one is shown on page 91) rather than 12 small ones.

CORN AND PANDAN BIBINGKAS

MAKES 8 TO 10 BIBINGKAS

INGREDIENTS

120 g	fine cornmeal
90 g	rice flour
30 g	tapioca starch
160 g	creamed corn
200 g	coconut milk
½ tsp	salt
8 to 12	pandan leaves (see pointers), washed
2	eggs
50 g	sugar
80 g	unsalted butter, melted
1¾ tsp	double-acting baking powder
	freshly grated coconut, lightly salted and chilled, to serve

EQUIPMENT

- a muffin or scone pan with 8 to 12 hollows (see pointers)

Corn, coconut and pandan form a lovely culinary conjunction. Corn and pandan share aroma notes reminiscent of freshly-popped corn and jasmine rice, while coconut's signature heady richness has natural affinities with pandan's vanilla-like and floral notes, and also corn's starchy sweetness. Together, the trio are as comely and unbeatable as Charlie's Angels.

Baking powder and an initial rest gives these cake-breads a light, fluffy texture much like that of modern wheat flour Filipino bibingkas, though they are wheat-free. Serve them hot, with chilled, lightly salted grated coconut, or with stews and mild curries, grilled sausages, and soups.

METHOD

1 To break up any lumps, sift cornmeal, rice flour and tapioca starch into a mixing bowl. Add creamed corn, coconut milk and salt, and whisk to make a thick, pasty batter. Cover bowl and let stand for 3 to 4 hours at cool room temperature, or 4 to 5 hours in the fridge.

2 Preheat oven to 190°C. Place a shelf in the middle position.

3 Trim off the thick, inflexible bases of the pandan leaves. Lightly grease your muffin or scone pans, then bend a pandan leaf to line the sides of each hollow, overlapping the ends by several centimetres. The natural springiness of the leaf should hold it in place.

4 Combine eggs and sugar in a mixing bowl. Whisk hard for 1 minute, by hand or with a mixer, until thick and frothy. Scrape cornmeal mixture into bowl and whisk to combine, then add melted butter and whisk hard for another 15 seconds. Sift in baking powder and whisk for another 15 seconds.

5 Pour the batter into pans. It should come up to 4 or 5 mm below the rims of the pandan leaves. Some of it may seep outside the leaves—no big deal. Bake for 20 to 25 minutes, until risen and browned, and an inserted cake tester emerges damp but clean. Do not overbake or bibingka will be dry.

6 Serve hot, with chilled, lightly salted grated coconut. They are best eaten within 2 days of baking—leftovers should be steamed to reheat before serving.

POINTERS

- Pandan leaves, also called screwpine or pandanus, look like giant blades of grass. They smell mildly vegetal when fresh and unmolested, only releasing their sweet aroma once subjected to heat or physical breakdown. They are tied into knots and used to infuse liquid dishes, cut and folded into containers or wrappings for food, or pounded with water and strained to yield a green juice for scenting and tinting desserts.
- Use very fine cornmeal for the lightest texture.
- Straight-sided scone or muffin pans are easier to line with the pandan leaves—I like to use the eight-wedge, circular pan shown here.
- These go well with young, crumbly-moist cheeses like Wensleydale or Lancashire.

TRACKS OF OUR TIERS

Is there anything as instantly addictive as pastry that shatters into crispy, flaky, buttery shards? Or as magical as making it yourself from scratch, and watching the oven transform pale dough into golden folios?

This is how dough lamination works: first, mix up a wheat flour dough containing enough water to help the flour proteins form a strong but extensible network. Then, mix up another dough chiefly composed of fat. Layer the two doughs in many alternating strata. When the final dough is baked or fried, the water in it turns to steam, and trapped air expands, both of which push the dough layers apart. Meanwhile, the fat melts, keeping the layers separate and crisping their outermost edges.

The earliest laminated dough recipes appear in medieval Arabic texts, which preserve many courtly dishes from Al-Andalus (the region of Spain and Portugal during the Moorish era). Scholars conjecture that from there, the techniques spread northwards and eastwards along land and sea trade routes. Certainly, laminated pastry recipes old enough to be considered traditional in their respective countries are today found across Western and Eastern Europe, Central Asia, China, India, some way into Southeast Asia, and Latin America. Here is a brief and far from exhaustive compendium, organised by method.

An early recipe, from a 13th-century Andalusian cookbook, details a spiral lamination technique: well-kneaded dough is thinly stretched, smeared evenly with pure melted fat, then rolled up tightly as one would a Swiss roll, forming a log with a spiralling internal layer structure. This foundation persists today in the following pastries:

SFOGLIATELLE

From Naples. Uniformly rolled water dough is brushed with butter and/or lard. The laminated log is sliced thickly; each slice is telescoped out into a cone shape, filled with a thick semolina custard flavoured with citrus and cinnamon, and baked.

SAMSA

Uzbekistan's distant kin to Indian samosas, made with water dough stretched wafer-thin, and lamb fat. Each log slice is rolled into a disc and topped with meat or vegetable filling. Three edges are folded to the centre, sealed together, and the triangular parcel baked seam-side down. The same dough, spiral laminated into a thicker log, sliced and rolled out plate-size, then fried or baked, becomes hundred-leafed Uzbek katlama bread.

CONG YOU BING

Chinese pancakes. Thinly rolled water dough is smeared with fat (lard, oil or shortening, often mixed with flour), sprinkled with chopped spring onions, and rolled up. The log is coiled horizontally into a disc (like a mosquito coil), flattened, and pan-fried.

—

Right, from top: *Italian sfogliatelle; Uzbek samsa; Uzbek katlama bread.* ***Opposite, from top:*** *a large chiroti species; a French puff pastry lattice; Cantonese egg custard tart.*

Another medieval Andalusian technique rolls dough into multiple separate sheets, which are spread with fat and stacked up one on another. These items start with that cue:

DAR NI PORI

A classic Parsi recipe. White-flour water dough circles are smeared with maan, a ghee and rice flour mix. They are stacked, then spiral laminated. Thick log slices are rolled into large discs, wrapped around a sweet and spiced mashed toor dal filling to make frisbee-size pastries, and griddle-fried.

CHIROTI

South Indian snacks, made from dough stacked and spiral laminated as is done for dar ni pori. Log slices are flattened into rounds or ovals, deep-fried, and glazed or sprinkled with sugar. Similar snacks are made in Nepal.

KARIPAP LAPIS

Traditional Malay curry puffs. ('Lapis' = layer.) Read on for my recipe (page 102).

—

Another European method, dating back at least as far as the Renaissance, wraps the mass of solid fat dough in the water dough, then rolls the package into a flat sheet, which is then laminated with 'turns'—three- or four-ply folds, as you would fold a letter. Thus are made two iconic recipes:

CLASSIC FRENCH PUFF PASTRY

The water dough encases the beurrage (a fat dough made of butter plus a little flour) like an envelope, the parcel then laminated with sufficient turns to yield several hundred layers. The butter's 20 per cent water content takes the puff to magnificent heights.

CHINESE PUFF PASTRY

This differs from French puff pastry by virtue of using lard, not butter. It expands less when baked, but remains melt-in-the-mouth flaky. Used for Cantonese egg custard tarts.

—

If such wrapped-and-rolled doughs are then laminated spirally instead of with turns, one gets the substrates for these next items:

TAU SAR PIAH

Chinese pastries popular in Singapore and Malaysia. Individual portions of water and lard doughs are wrapped and rolled out, then spiral laminated, rotated 90 degrees, flattened and spiral laminated a second time. The petite log is lastly flattened, then wrapped around sweetened mung bean paste to make a pastry the size and shape of a yo-yo, and baked. Curiously similar to a small dar ni pori—am I the first to notice this?

SPIRAL MOONCAKES

Various versions are made in Chaozhou, Suzhou, and the southern Chinese diaspora, with water and lard doughs. The log slices are rolled into discs, then wrapped around fillings as you would shape conventional stuffed buns. They bake up with well-defined laminations. A shaping variation that makes the striations run in parallel across the entire pastry is used in Cantonese dim sum.

PASTEL GULUNG/KARIPAP PUSING

Indonesian/Malay spiral curry puffs made with water and shortening doughs. The log slices are rolled into discs, topped with filling, folded into half-moons, crimped to seal and deep-fried until very crisp. Similar puffs with sweet fillings called karanji are made in south India.

And finally, one of the trickiest of all pastries and confections to perfect:

PASTEL DE NATA

Portuguese egg tarts, from Belém, Lisbon. A water dough is daubed with lard or shortening, given a couple of turns, then thinly rolled, spiral laminated, and thickly sliced. Each slice is pressed out to line a tart tin, using both thumbs in a quick spreading-fanning-rotating motion. The laminations are clearly visible (page 96) around the tart's rim after baking. The filling is an achingly sweet custard, dusted with cinnamon—very moreish, and Moorish.

I have distilled ideas and technique points gleaned from all the above in the following recipes, the first illustrating fold lamination, the second spiral lamination.

Clockwise from far left, top: *tau sar piah; radish pastries with parallel-striation shaping of spiral laminated dough; Indonesian pastel gulung; making tau sar piah pastry—at right, portioned-out fat dough blobs sit atop water dough discs, waiting to be wrapped and rolled.*

MAKES 8 PUFFS

INGREDIENTS

Beef rendang filling

10	shallots, peeled and sliced
8	garlic cloves, peeled and sliced
10	dried chillies, deseeded if desired, soaked till soft
2½ tbsp	finely chopped lemongrass
2 tbsp	minced peeled galangal
1 tbsp	minced peeled ginger
1 tsp	minced fresh turmeric
2 tbsp	ground coriander
1½ tsp	ground cumin
1 tsp	salt
¾ tsp	black pepper
750 g	coconut milk
700 g	stewing beef, cut into 3cm cubes
35 g	palm sugar, finely chopped
1 tbsp	kicap manis or thick dark soy sauce
2 tsp	lime juice
6	kaffir lime leaves

Water dough

500 g	plain flour, plus additional for dusting
1 tsp	ground turmeric
1 tsp	salt
150 g	cold unsalted butter, diced
150 g	cold water
1	egg

Fat dough

125 g	rendered beef fat (page 15)
40 g	rice flour
1	beaten egg, for glazing

EQUIPMENT

- a blender or spice grinder
- a baking sheet lined with baking paper
- patience

BEEF RENDANG KARIPAP LAPIS

Modern ready-made karipap are often unnaturally yellow and cellophane-crisp from pastry margarine, which is easy to work with in tropical weather, but has a gross, waxy mouthfeel. I have based my karipap on traditional recipes I found in 1970s Malay newspaper clippings. They are amazingly similar to medieval templates, wherein the dough is laminated with rendered beef fat (you could also use strained, solidified dripping from a roast beef joint). Its well-defined layers don't puff much, but have crisp edges and a full flavour.

METHOD

1 Make the filling. Combine first 11 ingredients (shallots through pepper) in a blender or spice grinder and grind to a very fine paste. Combine paste with all remaining filling ingredients in a large pot. Bring everything to a boil over medium heat. Cover pot, leaving lid ajar. Adjust heat to maintain a steady gentle boil, and cook for 1½ to 2 hours, stirring frequently, until the beef has fallen apart into tender shreds coated with a thick, clinging gravy. Adjust seasoning with more salt, sugar or lime juice as needed. Let cool.

2 Make water dough. Sift plain flour and turmeric into a mixing bowl. Add salt and whisk well to mix. Add butter and rub it in with your fingertips until it has completely dispersed and mixture looks like fine crumbs. Beat water and egg together until blended, pour over flour mixture and stir with a spatula until dough comes together. Knead it briefly just to even out the moisture. Wrap dough tightly in plastic wrap and chill for at least 1 hour.

3 Make fat dough. Combine fat and rice flour in a bowl and stir until evenly combined. Cover bowl with plastic wrap and chill until firmed up and spreadable.

4 Unwrap water dough and cut it into quarters. Place a large sheet of baking paper on a work surface, and dust with flour. Roll out one water dough portion into a 30 cm square. With a palette knife, spread one-third of the fat dough mixture evenly over the water dough square, leaving a 0.5 cm margin all around.

5 Roll out another portion of water dough to a 30 cm square, then place it on top of the first one. Spread with half the remaining fat dough. Repeat the rolling, stacking and spreading until both doughs are used up, and you have a square stack of 4 water dough layers interspersed with 3 fat dough layers. Wrap the stack up in the baking paper. Chill for 1 hour.

6 Unwrap stack. Dust it on both sides with flour. Roll it out to a large square, about 40 cm across. Fold the top third down, and then the bottom third up over it, as you'd fold a business letter. Press to flatten slightly, then fold the strip in half, left to right. Rewrap the resulting chubby slab in the baking paper and chill for 1 hour.

7 Preheat oven to 210°C. Place a shelf in the middle position.

8 Unwrap the dough. Roll it out on a well-floured work surface to a large rectangle, about 50 cm long and 40 cm wide. Cut it into four 40 cm-long strips, then cut each strip across into half to make 8 rectangles.

9 Place 4 to 5 tablespoons of filling on the bottom half of a rectangle, leaving a 1 cm margin. Moisten the margin with a wet fingertip, then fold the top half down to cover the filling. Press around the edge to seal, then trim edges. Make all puffs likewise. Place them on the baking sheet, spacing them about 2.5 cm apart.

10 Brush the puffs with beaten egg, but don't let it drip down their sides or it will interfere with the puffing. Bake for 20 to 30 minutes, until risen and well browned.

11 Serve warm or at room temperature. Best eaten within 2 days of baking. Reheat to serve.

MAKES 16 PASTRIES

INGREDIENTS

Water dough

40 g	water
1	egg yolk
15 g	icing sugar
¼ tsp	fine salt
100 g	plain flour, plus additional for dusting
25 g	bread flour
55 g	cold unsalted butter, diced

Fat dough

100 g	cake flour
50 g	rendered duck fat (see pointers), well chilled and firm
	one batch of either filling (recipes follow)

EQUIPMENT

- long and short rolling pins (page 17)
- a baking sheet lined with baking paper
- patience

POINTERS

- Look for cans or jars of rendered duck fat at gourmet food shops. It keeps for 1 to 2 months in the fridge or freezer once opened. You can use lard or goose fat instead.
- Keep the raw pastry cool and dry at all times. Use as little flour as possible to prevent it sticking to the work surface, rolling pin and your hands. Dampness from condensation will glue the layers together, thwarting the lamination.
- Do not stress. The lamination process is much easier to do than to describe, and not difficult to get the hang of.

SPIRAL PASTRIES

These pastries owe their featheriness to duck fat, whose light and neutral taste is perfectly apt for both sweet and savoury fillings.

METHOD

1 Make water dough. Whisk water, egg yolk, sugar and salt together until salt dissolves. Set aside. Sift plain flour and bread flour into a bowl. Add butter, and rub it in with your fingertips until evenly dispersed and mixture resembles fine sand. Pour in water mixture and stir with a spatula to bring dough together. With the spatula, gently squash and fold it back on itself 4 to 6 times, to even it out and work its gluten. Wrap dough tightly in plastic wrap and chill for at least 1 hour.

2 Make fat dough. Sift cake flour into a bowl, add duck fat and stir in to make a soft, putty-like dough. Wrap tightly in plastic wrap and chill for at least 1 hour.

3 Unwrap water dough, place on a flour-dusted surface, and press it out into a rectangle. Press out fat dough into a rectangle half as wide as the water dough, and lay it on top of the water dough. Fold over the water dough to wrap and enclose the fat dough, pressing them flushly together so that no air is trapped. Press all seams to seal. Gently, evenly roll out the parcel into an oblong about 30 cm by 40 cm. Fold the top third down, and then the bottom third up over it, as you'd fold a business letter. Fold the left third in, then the right third over that. You now have a 9-ply chubby pastry slab. Wrap in plastic wrap and chill for 45 minutes so that it (and you) can relax.

4 Unwrap slab. Dust it well with flour. Roll it out to a rectangle about 25 cm by 45 cm. Brush off any excess flour. Starting at a short end, roll it up tightly, like a Swiss roll. Wrap cylinder in plastic wrap and chill for 1 hour or until completely firm.

5 Preheat oven to 200°C. Place a shelf in the lower third of the oven.

6 Lightly oil a very sharp, thin-bladed knife. Trim cylinder ends, then cut cylinder into 16 equal slices.

7 With the heel of your hand, press down on a slice, pushing from its centre to its edge to flatten it slightly; rotate it as you go, pressing 4 or 5 times in total. Next, with a short rolling pin, roll strokes from the centre of the disc out to its edge, flattening and extending the pastry; between strokes, rotate the disc with your other hand. (I roll away from myself with my right hand, while rotating the disc anti-clockwise with my left hand.) You should need 6 to 8 strokes to return to your starting point. If the disc is not thin enough after one round, go around one more time, but no more—excess pressure will weld the layers together, ruining the lamination. The finished disc should be 2 to 3 mm thick, slightly thinner at its rim than at its centre, and 10 to 12 cm in diameter.

8 Place a ball of bean or meat filling on the disc's centre. Wrap the dough flush around the filling without trapping any air, making gathers just as you would wrap a dumpling. Pinch to seal. Place pastry sealed side down on the baking sheet; the spiral laminations will be faintly visible on its upper surface. Make all pastries likewise (see photos overleaf).

9 Bake *sweet* bean pastries for 20 to 23 minutes, until pale golden. Serve warm or at room temperature. They will stay lightly crisp for a few days, kept in an airtight container in the fridge—warm them in a toaster oven to serve, if desired.

10 Bake *savoury* meat pastries for 23 to 25 minutes, until well browned. Serve them hot. Their shells soften as they cool and will only partially re-crisp on reheating.

11 For *both pastries*, turn the baking sheet around front to back after the first 10 minutes of baking, to help the pastries colour evenly.

***This page, top row, left to right**: wrapping fat dough in water dough and rolling it out (Step 3). **Middle row, left to right:** folding two turns (step 3). **Bottom row, left to right:** the 9-ply slab; rolling slab out; rolling it up (Step 4). **Opposite page, top row, left to right:** the rolled-up log; a slice; flattening the slice (Step 7). **Second row, left to right:** rolling out the slice (Step 7); wrapping momo filling up (Step 8). **Bottom left:** underside and top of the shaped spiral momo. **Bottom right:** baked spiral momo.*

SWEET MAPLE BEAN PASTE FILLING

MAKES ENOUGH FOR 16 PASTRIES

INGREDIENTS

800 g	canned butter beans (see pointers)
180 g	maple syrup, preferably Grade A dark
35 g	unsalted butter
⅓ tsp	salt (see pointers)

POINTERS

- Adjust the salt amount depending on how much the beans already contain, and how sweet your tooth is. I start with beans canned in unsalted water, and add just enough salt to poise the paste perfectly between sweet and savoury.

Commercial Chinese tau sar piah (mung bean pastries) have fillings often over-laden with oil and sugar. My streamlined alternative features satiny butter beans and a touch of maple.

METHOD

1 Drain and rinse the butter beans. Remove their skins—this is tedious, but yields a much smoother paste. The easiest way to do it is to break each bean in half and gently squeeze to pop the halves out of their skins. Mash beans finely with a fork. You should have 375 to 400 g of mash.

2 Combine maple syrup, butter and salt in a frying pan and bring to a simmer over medium heat. Add beans. Stir, mash and fold constantly with a heatproof spatula, until the slurry thickens into a fine beige paste with the texture of smooth mashed potatoes. This should take 6 to 9 minutes. Transfer paste to a bowl and let cool completely. Cover bowl tightly and chill paste until needed. It will keep for 2 to 3 days, refrigerated.

MAKES ENOUGH FOR 16 PASTRIES

INGREDIENTS

450 g	minced pork, beef or chicken, preferably slightly fatty
20 g	finely chopped fresh coriander leaves
50 g	finely minced onion
2 tsp	grated garlic
2 tsp	grated ginger
2 tsp	finely minced fresh green chilli
1¾ tsp	ground coriander
¾ tsp	ground cumin
¾ tsp	fine salt, or to taste
½ tsp	finely ground black pepper
½ tsp	chilli powder
½ tsp	ground turmeric
	potato starch, for dusting

SAVOURY MOMO FILLING

A tribute to the momo dumplings I used to inhale by the dozen (six steamed, six fried) at Everest Kitchen, my favourite Nepali restaurant. The baked momo crusts have a semi-soft, semi-crisp texture similar to Uzbek samsa.

METHOD

1 Combine all ingredients except potato starch in a bowl and stir together to blend without compacting the mixture too much—chopsticks or fingers are the best at this.

2 Only just before you shape and bake the pastries, divide and shape the filling into 16 balls. Roll them lightly in potato starch to coat—this helps to seal in and retain their juices, guarding against leaks through the pastry shells.

POINTERS

- For a Nepali-style achar (fresh chutney) to go with momos, grind 60 g fresh coriander leaves, 75 g diced tomato, 1 hot green chilli, 1 clove garlic, 2 teaspoons minced ginger, 1 teaspoon toasted sesame seeds, and salt and lemon juice to taste together in a pestle and mortar, or a blender.

CRUST-WORTHY

I wonder, who was the first person to bake one dough atop another?

The technique produces striking effects and textural contrasts well known to Asian bun fanatics. The buns pictured overleaf have long been mainstays in Asian bakeries, and I always assumed that they were from around here. But as it turns out, their ancestry is probably Hispanic. (The exception, which I have included out of interest and for contrast, is the Dutch crunch bun—its topping suggests a kinship with rustic European breads like Alsatian pain à la bière.)

In Mexico, wheat bread traditions began with the introduction of the grain after the Spanish conquest, diversifying to include plain loaves and pan dulce (sweet breads) by the late 1500s. French influences and convent-created innovations subsequently elaborated the national repertoire, which expanded further after the Mexican Revolution. Today, traditional panaderías (bakeries) make a truly vast range of breads, cakes, biscuits, pastries and hybrids of all of these, most with vivid shapes and names—volcanoes, crocodiles, skulls, seashells and the like. Among the two-dough varieties, buns called picones ('coals') from Guadalajara are virtually identical to bor lor bau, topped with a lard or shortening crust that crazes in the oven. A paler, sugar-dusted pan dulce called nube ('cloud') is a twin of melon pan.

Waves of Chinese and Japanese emigrants entered Mexico from the late 1800s, many brought in to work in mines and on railroads, some looking for a new life. Many Chinese who settled there permanently started food businesses—Chinese cafes serving both Mexican and Chinese food were fixtures in Mexico City by the 1940s. The Mexico bun was reportedly invented in the late 1940s by Chinese entrepreneurs who moved back to Hong Kong from Mexico, opening the Mexico Bing Sutt (meaning cafe-diner) to sell their pan dulce-inspired creation.

While their details are lost to time, it seems wholly probable, if not inevitable, that bor lor bau and melon pan have similar origin stories. The spiral bun may descend from a novia ('bride') pan dulce, named for its wedding-dress vibe. Permit me to also note that the little pastry pigs enjoyed during the Chinese Mid-Autumn Festival are tellingly similar in shape and makeup to Mexican cookies named puerquitos, cochinitos or marranitos, all meaning 'piglet'. And in fact, the self-service style of Asian bakeries—collate your own tray of items and bring them to the till to pay—is traditional to Mexican panaderías. Son of a bun.

Bor lor bau ('pineapple bun' in Cantonese)

A plain bun topped with a thick hat of sweet lard cookie dough, grid-scored to resemble a stylised pineapple, that bakes up crackly and crumbly. Variations may include fillings such as char siu (roasted pork). From Hong Kong.

Mexico bun

A tuile cookie-like paste (a coffee variation is shown here) is piped onto the custard-filled bun, spreading during baking to envelop it in a uniform thin, sweet, friable layer. From Hong Kong.

Melon pan

A plain bun completely covered with sweet cookie dough, dusted with coarse sugar. Originally scored with parallel lines, now more often a grid, both in imitation of grooves on a real melon. From Japan.

Chocolate melon pan

A variation with a cocoa cookie crust. Other variations boast crust flavours like green tea, and sweet or savoury fillings.

Spiral bun

Topped with a thin slice of tightly-coiled puff pastry. Seen in both Chinese and Japanese bakeries.

Dutch crunch roll, a.k.a. tiger roll

Plain bread dough, painted with a yeasted rice flour batter that bakes up into crisp, giraffe-pattern flakes. From Holland.

MAKES 16 BUNS

INGREDIENTS

Topping

115 g	plain flour
10 g	rice flour
20 g	sugar
⅓ tsp	salt
20 g	fresh curry leaves, washed and stems removed
20 g	curry roux, crumbled
30 g	cold unsalted butter, diced
⅓ tsp	ammonium bicarbonate (page 16)
2 tsp	water
1	egg

Dough

240 g	boiling water
60 g	curry roux, crumbled finely
60 g	sugar
30 g	unsalted butter
15 g	milk powder
¼ tsp	salt
400 g	bread flour
1½ tsp	instant yeast (page 15)
1	egg

EQUIPMENT

- a blender or food processor
- a stand mixer fitted with the dough hook
- a baking sheet lined with baking paper

JAPANESE CURRY MELON PAN

Sweet melon pan walk on the mild side, but these savoury melon pan have a (polite) kick from a very Japanese ingredient: curry roux. Anglo-Indian curries were reputedly introduced to Japan by the British Navy in the 1800s, and quickly propagated through military and institutional kitchens before gaining ground in restaurants. A pre-cooked blend of fat, flour, spices and condiments, curry roux was created in the 1950s, and rapidly became an enormously popular home pantry staple: you simply dissolve it into a pot of broth and cooked ingredients to reconstitute the curry. Curry roux adds pre-gelatinised starch (page 135) to the soft crumb of these pan, and also flavour to their crumbly topping.

METHOD

1 Make the topping. Combine flour, rice flour, sugar, salt, curry leaves and curry roux in a blender and pulse-blend until leaves are finely ground. Add butter and pulse until it disperses and mixture looks like fine crumbs. Tip mixture into a bowl. Whisk ammonium bicarbonate with water to dissolve it, then beat in the egg. Pour into dry ingredients and mix to a soft dough. Wrap dough in plastic wrap and chill for 1 hour, until firm.

2 Make the dough. Whisk boiling water and curry roux together in a bowl until roux dissolves, then add sugar, butter, milk powder and salt and whisk until smooth. Let cool completely.

3 Whisk bread flour and yeast together in a mixing bowl. Add curry mixture and egg and mix on low speed until dough comes together into a ball. Cover bowl with a damp tea towel and let dough rest for 30 minutes.

4 Knead the dough on medium-low speed for 1 minute. Re-cover bowl with the tea towel and let dough rest for 5 minutes. Repeat the kneading and resting once more. Finally, knead for 1 to 2 minutes, until the dough is elastic and starts to clean bowl sides. Re-cover bowl and let stand at cool room temperature until dough has doubled in size, about 70 to 90 minutes.

5 Rub your hands and the work surface lightly with oil. Turn out the dough and press it gently all over to deflate it, then divide it into 16 portions. Shape each into a tight, compact round ball by cupping it under your oiled palm and dragging it in small circles on the work surface. Place dough balls on the paper-lined baking sheet, spaced about 4 cm apart. Cover with greased plastic wrap and let proof at cool room temperature until just doubled in size, about 30 to 40 minutes.

6 Preheat oven to 190°C. Place a shelf in the middle position.

7 While buns proof, divide topping into 16 portions and roll each into a ball. Dust a ball lightly with flour, sandwich it between two small sheets of baking paper, and roll it into a thin disc about 8 cm in diameter. Peel off top paper sheet. Lift the dough on the bottom sheet, and invert it over the top of a risen bun. Gently pat it flush against the bun, so it hugs it all round. Peel off paper. Drape all buns with topping likewise.

8 Bake the buns for 15 minutes, until the topping has crazed and lightly browned, and bun undersides are golden brown.

9 Transfer baking sheet to a rack. Let buns cool slightly, then serve warm with butter. They go well with creamy vegetable soups, and make great beds—futons?—for burgers. Best eaten within a day of baking, as the topping eventually softens.

POINTERS

- Fresh curry leaves brighten the topping with their warm peppery-citric fragrance.
- Japanese curry roux is sold in boxed blocks at Japanese supermarts. Its considerable slew of ingredients may include fruit, such as banana or apple, peanut butter for creaminess, cheese for more umami, as well as animal fats like lard or beef dripping, so read labels carefully if you have allergies or other objections to such. 'Java-style' curry roux, which tends to be spicier, suits these buns well.

MAKES 16 BUNS

PANDAN PÃO DE DEUS

Could pão de Deus ('bread of God') be another precursor of two-dough buns? Maybe or maybe not, but they're too heavenly to leave out of the discussion. These traditional Portuguese treats are capped with eggy, sugary coconut goo, like a luxurious macaroon batter—over the top in all senses. I've reined in the richness a bit to better frame a pandan-infused dough, pandan and coconut being a favourite Asian pairing. My mouth waters just at the thought of these.

INGREDIENTS

Dough

15	pandan leaves (page 94)
180 g	water
2	egg yolks
20 g	potato starch
60 g	caster sugar
6 g	(1 scant teaspoon) salt
240 g	bread flour
100 g	plain flour
1¼ tsp	osmotolerant or regular instant yeast (page 15)
1	egg white
35 g	unsalted butter, diced and slightly softened
35 g	coconut cream
	oil, for shaping

Topping

2	egg whites
70 g	caster sugar
¾ tsp	potato starch
35 g	salted butter, melted and cooled
200 g	grated fresh coconut
2	egg yolks

EQUIPMENT

- a stand mixer fitted with the dough hook
- a baking sheet lined with baking paper

METHOD

1 Blend pandan leaves with water in a blender until leaves resemble grass clippings. Strain through a very fine sieve; press on leaves to extract as much green juice as possible. Measure out 180 g of the juice, making it up with water if necessary.

2 Combine pandan juice, egg yolks, potato starch, sugar and salt in a small pot and set over medium-low heat. Whisk constantly until mixture thickens into a gloopy custard. Scrape mixture into a bowl and let cool completely.

3 Whisk both flours and yeast together in a mixing bowl. Add cooled pandan custard and egg white, and stir with a spatula to make a soft dough. Cover bowl with a damp tea towel and let it stand at room temperature for 30 minutes.

4 Knead dough for 1 minute on medium speed. Re-cover bowl and let dough rest for 10 minutes. Repeat the kneading and resting once. Finally, add butter and coconut cream to bowl and knead for a final 3 minutes on medium-low speed, until they have been absorbed—it will be sloppy going at first—and the dough has smoothened out again, and just starts to clean the bowl sides.

5 Scrape dough into a clean bowl lightly greased with oil, cover it, and let it stand at room temperature until risen to double its original size, about 1 hour.

6 Rub your hands and the work surface lightly with oil. Turn out the dough and press it gently all over to deflate it, then divide it into 16 portions. Shape each into a tight, compact round ball by cupping it under your oiled palm and dragging it in small circles on your floured work surface. Place balls on the baking sheet, spacing them about 4 cm apart. Place them in your turned-off oven, shut the door and let them rise until doubled in size, about 1 hour.

POINTERS

- If you can't get grated fresh coconut, use desiccated coconut. Sprinkle it well with water and let it rehydrate for a few minutes until evenly moist, then weigh it out.
- I deliberately leave the topping a bit rough, for a contrast between crunchy browned bits and moister shreds underneath. For a smoother slab of topping, add 2 tablespoons coconut cream to the mixture, and spoon/pat it on more carefully.
- Do as the Portuguese do and stuff a split pão with a thin slice of ham —the salty-sweet combination is really delicious.

7 Make the topping. Combine egg whites with sugar, potato starch and melted butter, and whisk until smooth. Fold in the grated coconut. Cover tightly until needed.

8 Take the buns out of the oven. Preheat oven to 180°C. Place a shelf in the middle position.

9 Beat the egg yolks together to blend, then brush very lightly all over the risen buns. Stir the topping well, then pat a thick but even mound of it onto the top of each bun, gently, so as to not deflate it.

10 Bake for 18 to 21 minutes, until well browned. Buns may grow together as they rise and bake—this is fine.

11 Transfer baking sheet to a rack to cool. Serve buns warm or at room temperature.

THE BANHMICLAIR

Craquelin choux puffs, whose berets of shortbread dough bake up into crisp domes (pages 110 and 153), are now de rigueur in Paris. If I remember correctly, however, they first appeared in Asian bakeries, in the late 1990s. I'd since wondered if other toppings than craquelin were possible. Some days after I'd been mulling over Vietnamese dishes for various projects—and, frankly, agitated from post-Cronut franken-dessert splicery trends—I was struck by a fully-formed vision of The Banhmiclair. The flour batter glazing the choux batons bakes up crisp and crackly like a baguette crust, making them fine mini-vessels for banh mi fillings. Thank you, Viet baking muse.

A classic Vietnamese banh mi is a baguette filled with steamed, roasted or grilled filllings, including meat, cold cuts, pâté, seafood or vegetarian options. This is further festooned with crunchy pickles, cucumber, sliced chilli, coriander leaf sprigs, butter or mayo, and a salty-tangy seasoning sauce. The ensuing taste and textural contrasts lift the whole sandwich to nirvana.

MAKES 18 TO 20 BANHMICLAIRS

INGREDIENTS

Choux pastry

100 g	plain flour
25 g	bread flour
120 g	water
90 g	milk
90 g	unsalted butter
1 tsp	sugar
½ tsp	salt
2	eggs whites
3	eggs

Glaze

15 g	bread flour
10 g	rice flour
40 g	water
⅛ tsp	instant yeast (page 15)

Quick-pickled carrot

1 large	carrot
½ tsp	fine salt
3 tbsp	water
2 tbsp	rice vinegar
1 tbsp	caster sugar

Seasoning sauce

1 tbsp	fish sauce
1½ tsp	light soy sauce
1½ tsp	dark brown sugar

Other accompaniments, to taste

mayonnaise or butter
pâté, cold cuts, sliced roast meats
julienned peeled cucumber
fresh coriander leaves
sliced red chilli

EQUIPMENT

- 2 baking sheets lined with baking paper
- a piping bag fitted with a 1.5 cm-wide plain round piping tip
- a pastry brush
- a julienne cutter or a box grater

METHOD

1 Using the ingredients listed above, make choux pastry dough exactly as for the Choux Tourteaux (page 152). Pay especial attention when adding the last egg, and do not add too much of it—the choux dough should be thick enough that the banhmiclairs barely sag at all after being piped. Fill the piping bag with the dough and twist to seal.

2 Preheat oven to 195°C.
Place shelves in the upper and lower third of the oven. Have your paper-lined baking sheets ready.

3 Make the glaze just before piping the choux. Whisk all ingredients together in a small bowl. Cover and let stand for 10 minutes while you pipe the choux.

4 Pipe choux dough batons about 10 to 12 cm long, spacing them about 4 cm apart on the baking paper. Brush batons with a thin but even layer of glaze; it should not flow all the way down to the baking paper on both sides. (If it is too runny, add a bit more rice flour.) With the tip of a skewer, score a shallow lengthwise groove down the middle of each baton.

5 Dip your fingertips in a bowl of water and sprinkle droplets of water all over the baking sheets—this will create humidity in the oven, aiding the puffing. Bake batons for 20 minutes. Reduce heat to 175°C (without opening oven) and bake for 10 minutes. Swap baking sheets around, and bake for 5 to 10 minutes more, until batons are crisp and dry. Transfer baking sheets to racks to cool.

6 Pickle the carrot while the batons bake. Scrub carrot and cut into long juliennes. Place in a bowl, sprinkle with the salt, and gently massage it into the carrot with your fingers for 1 minute. Let stand for 10 minutes, then drain, rinse and drain again. Stir water, vinegar and sugar together to dissolve sugar, then stir in carrot juliennes. Cover and let stand for 15 to 25 minutes. Drain well before using.

7 Make the seasoning sauce by simply stirring all its ingredients together.

8 To assemble the Banhmiclairs: halve each choux baton horizontally. Spread a dab of mayo or butter inside both halves, then sprinkle with a few drops of seasoning sauce. Spread the bottom half with your chosen filling, then top with drained pickled carrot julienne, cucumber, coriander sprigs and sliced chillies. Place upper half of baton on top. Serve immediately.

POINTERS

- Most fun for all and least work for you: lay out all the fillings and accompaniments and let diners assemble their own banhmiclairs.
- Maggi Seasoning is the sauce most often used in orthodox banh mi, but I find it a little too strident, hence my homemade substitute.
- In the photos I have used two kinds of pork-based pâté, one fine and one coarse.

Chicken Roll
Bánh Mì Gà
Nước Sót Me
$4.00
Pork Roll
Bánh Mì Thịt
$3.00

3.

TREKS & THOUGHTS

Some people are perpetual motion machines: they bound and rebound against the limits of their tethers. Others prefer stasis as default, gravitating to equilibrium like a tea leaf to a cup bottom.

In my life, journeys and migrations have more often been imposed than chosen, so I often find myself divided. I constantly hunger to fill not just belly but also eyes, ears and spirit, and so my mind says "explore!", but my heart says "stay put with a cup of tea and a bacon roll, if possible". Reflecting this tussle between the unknown and the safe is my travel kit: camera, notebook, pen, folding maps, dental floss, ginger tea potent enough to quash internal disturbance of any kind, alcohol wipes. Rising above the discord is the kit's most essential but invisible component, which holds true whatever a journey or an oven may throw at you—the understanding that all which is gratefully received, is gift.

AMERICA

I first learnt about American food not from cookbooks, but from prose. The pie-centric reveries and dairy raptures of Farmer Boy, from the Little House series by Laura Ingalls Wilder, engrossed me to the point of trance. So would random vignettes: Harriet The Spy's tomato sandwiches, Miss Maudie's lane cake in *To Kill A Mockingbird*, Annie Dillard's coffee purposefully brewed to sustain a writer's toils.

Whereas the food in the British kids' books I also devoured often had a dutiful air—the Famous Five's lashings-of-boiled-eggs blowouts read a bit like wartime deprivation fantasies—American authors' ruminations had an appealing, vivid largesse. I unconsciously emulated it in my own writing. My secondary-school English teacher (who was British) once remarked that my essay style wasn't so much cerebral as more—he paused to pick the word—"... sensuous." God bless you, Mr Roberts—it chafed, for I wanted to be a scientist back then, but you were right.

Subsequent jaunts to the USA, through cookbook pages and (too seldom) in person, writ that largesse larger. When

I finally made it there, in a Gershwin-muzaked airport limo whose night-time cruise through Manhattan felt like foreplay, New York City won my heart. Old friends and new, so proud of their skyscrapered food capital, kindly took me out for herring in a Russian 'fur coat' of beets and eggs, fiery Latino shrimp with rice and beans, chunky Polish pierogis, and DiFara's pizza with hand-cut basil—this so soulful and good I almost wept, because my flight back the next day wouldn't let me return for another slice.

In 2007, I visited Napa Valley, to give talks as part of team Singapore at the Culinary Institute of America's Worlds of Flavor food congress.

I breathed deeply of vineyard air, watched Iron Chef Morimoto reduce students to starstruck giggles, tasted California-grown rambutans and shared a staff meal of retro-style pork shoulder baked with four kinds of citrus fruit and a litre of cola.

I didn't have the budget (or the contacts) to reach The French Laundry, but that was fine... Thomas Keller never made it to my grandma's table either, so the Force retains its balance.

Oh beautiful for spacious skies and portions, for pancake mountains empurpled with blueberries, for desserts packing as much butter and sugar as allowed by quantum physics into every cubic inch. In all its excesses, but also its straightforwardness, American baking tutors me in wrangling flavours, in knowing when to rein them in and when to let 'em thrillingly loose.

Left, top to bottom: *DiFara's pizza; Midwestern pumpkins; souvenirs from guess which city.* ***Opposite, clockwise from top left:*** *Katz's Deli pastrami sandwich; buffalo burger with a view, South Dakota; Napa Valley.*

MASALA BUTTERMILK OVEN-FRIED CHICKEN

I once went on a press junket through parts of the American Midwest. After several meals' worth of meat-and-potatoes bonhomie, and finally given a free evening, all us Asian journos made a beeline for the nearest supermarket to resolve our fruit and salad deficit. I kept getting side-tracked along the way: by the homewares section, where light weaponry and Varmint Hunter magazines sat alongside craft materials; by an entire aisle of potato chips; and by the deli counter's hot, crusty, thunder-thighed and buxom-breasted freshly fried chicken. I brought some back to my motel room to garnish my salad. It was bliss.

Fried chicken, my heart's desire and arteries' nemesis, how do I resist thee? Baking is a partial solution. In America, 'buttermilk' is a cultured product akin to runny yoghurt, much used in baking, and to marinate Southern fried chicken. In Singapore, 'buttermilk' is a refreshing savoury South Indian drink accented with curry leaves, ginger and pepper. This recipe brings the two worlds together, imbuing an American buttermilk soak and cornflake crust with Indian spices. A popular component of chivda and murukku (crispy snacks), masala cornflakes are sold at Indian supermarts. If you can't get them, just use regular cornflakes.

SERVES 4 TO 6

INGREDIENTS

1	small purple or red onion, peeled and chopped
4	garlic cloves, peeled and chopped
2	hot green chillies
2 tsp	minced ginger
2 tsp	sea salt
1 tsp	fennel seeds
1 tsp	cumin seeds
1 tsp	black peppercorns
½ tsp	ground turmeric
6 sprigs	curry leaves, stems removed
1 tbsp	Dijon mustard
500 g	buttermilk
10	chicken pieces on the bone (see pointers)
150 g	plain flour
250 g	masala cornflakes (roughly 4 cups)
75 g	panko breadcrumbs (roughly 1½ cups)
	oil, for greasing

EQUIPMENT

- a blender or food processor
- a large roasting pan
- a wire roasting rack

POINTERS

- I cut one chicken breast (from half a chicken) into two chunky pieces. Drumsticks and thighs I count as one piece each. Wings tend to end up having too little meat in proportion to the coating—a bonus for some diners, a minus for others.
- For a slightly crispier crust, spray the coated chicken pieces with oil before baking.

METHOD

1 Grind the first 9 ingredients (onion through turmeric) together into a fine paste in a blender or food processor. Add curry leaves and mustard and blend until leaves are ground into tiny bits. Scrape paste into a deep bowl and whisk in buttermilk, then add chicken pieces and mix well—they should be submerged. Cover and let marinate in the fridge for 4 to 5 hours.

2 Preheat oven to 190°C. Place a shelf in the lower third of the oven.

3 Line a large roasting pan with foil. Place a wire rack in the pan that stands at least 2.5 cm above the pan bottom, so that air can circulate around the chicken as it cooks. Grease the wire rack well with oil.

4 Spread flour out on a tray. Crush cornflakes into small crumbs with your hands, combine with panko, and spread out on another tray.

5 Wipe excess marinade off a chicken piece, then roll it in the flour to coat lightly. Dip it back in the marinade to coat thinly but thoroughly, and finally roll it in the cornflake mixture to coat well. Place it on the greased wire rack. Coat all chicken pieces likewise. Space them out at least 3 cm apart on the rack.

6 Bake the chicken for 45 to 50 minutes, until golden brown and cooked through. Depending on their size, breast pieces may be done slightly earlier, after about 35 to 40 minutes—if they are, remove them and put the drumsticks and thighs back in to finish cooking.

7 Serve the chicken piping hot. Leftovers can be oven-reheated, but don't let them dry out.

SPREADABLE PIES

A South Dakota diner. 7.30am frost on the windows. Old men with trucker caps nurse mugs of coffee strong enough to feel in your toes right after a sip. Maternal waitresses bustle. Face-sized pancakes are anointed with maple syrup, eggs are benedicted with shiny hollandaise. Contentment rises like coffee steam. I spy perfectly browned pies, tops sandy with sugar. I am full to the brim, but this is pie country—how can I pass them up? I order a slice of peach pie, mouth watering in anticipation.

Reader, it was awful.

Industrial peach filling gave that pie all the pizzazz (and mouthfeel) of tile grouting, but it did not shake my belief that a traditional pie made with love and intelligence is the apotheosis of baking craft and art. And yet, is America not the land of transformation and reboots, of reshaping reality through sheer force of will? Of spray-on cheese and jellied salads, where steak is fried like chicken and apples are made into butter? Ladies and gentlemen, I give you—spreadable pies.

INGREDIENTS

170 g	cake flour
30 g	plain flour
⅓ tsp	fine salt
110 g	cold unsalted butter, cut into small bits
1	egg, beaten

EQUIPMENT

- a food processor
- a rimmed baking tray lined with baking paper

PIE CRUST CRUMB BASE METHOD

1 Preheat oven to 170°C. Place a shelf in the middle position.

2 Combine cake flour, plain flour, salt and butter in the food processor, and pulse-blend until the mixture forms fine crumbs. Add egg and pulse until the dough comes together in clumps. (To mix the dough by hand, whisk the two flours and salt together, then rub in the butter with your fingertips, working quickly so the butter doesn't become soft and greasy. Beat the egg and stir in with a fork.)

3 Break up the clumps into small crumbs—the largest ones should be no bigger than peas—and strew them evenly across the baking tray. Bake for 25 to 30 minutes, stirring every 10 minutes, until crumbs are evenly golden all over. Transfer tray to a rack and let crumbs cool completely.

4 Pulse-blend the cooled crumbs in a food processor until finely pulverised—stop before they become a paste. Transfer to a resealable bag, press all the air out, and chill until needed. The crumbs keep for 2 to 3 days in the fridge.

SERVING SUGGESTIONS

What can you do with spreadable pies? What *can't* you do, honeychild?

- Daub them on plain, thin savoury biscuits—water biscuits, thin oatcakes, saltine-type crackers and such
- Spoon them over ice cream or Greek yoghurt
- Stir them into hot cereal, or cold cereal, for that matter
- Use them to flavour milkshakes
- Serve them as elements on a cheese and fruit platter
- Sandwich macarons with them
- Eat them straight out of the jar with your fingers

To make any of the following spreadable pies, which each yields a small jam jar's worth: whisk all the gooey ingredients together in a bowl, then stir in all the dry ingredients until blended. Transfer the spread to a sterilised jar and cover tightly. It will keep in the fridge for 3 to 5 days.

SPREADABLE APPLE PIE

You can use either red-skinned or green-skinned apple chips—look for them in supermarket snack aisles.

INGREDIENTS

75 g	crispy freeze-dried apple chips, finely crushed
50 g	pie crust crumbs
45 g	sweetened condensed milk
2 tsp	freshly squeezed lemon juice
1 tsp	honey
½ tsp	ground cinnamon

SPREADABLE LEMON MERINGUE PIE

Sprinkle the pearl sugar over or stir it in only just before serving, so it won't dissolve—its sweet crunch mimics that of meringue.

60 g	pie crust crumbs
125 g	prepared lemon curd
1 tsp	freshly squeezed lemon juice
⅛ tsp	vanilla extract

pearl sugar, for sprinkling

SPREADABLE PECAN PIE

For the most sublime results, make sure your pecans are really fresh.

70 g	pecans, toasted and finely chopped
50 g	pie crust crumbs
50 g	golden syrup or maple syrup
30 g	sweetened condensed milk
1 tsp	molasses
tiny pinch	fine salt

SPREADABLE BLUEBERRY PIE

For the best flavour, use blueberry jam made with at least 55 per cent fruit—or cook down fresh or frozen berries yourself—and marble it through rather than completely blending it in.

50 g	pie crust crumbs
50 g	sweetened condensed milk
1 tsp	freshly squeezed lemon juice
80 g	blueberry jam

SPREADABLE PUMPKIN PIE

To roast pumpkin, cut deseeded pumpkin into thin wedges, place on a baking tray, and roast at 180°C until tender and lightly browned at the edges.

110 g	pureed roasted pumpkin
50 g	pie crust crumbs
50 g	golden syrup or maple syrup
40 g	sweetened condensed milk
tiny pinch	fine salt
1 tsp	rum or bourbon
¼ tsp	pumpkin pie spice

SERVES 12 TO 16 NORMAL PEOPLE OR 4 GREEDY ONES

INGREDIENTS

Custard

185 g	water
25 g	powdered milk
2	egg yolks
30 g	potato starch
55 g	sugar
6 g	(1 scant teaspoon) salt
55 g	unsalted butter, diced
330 g	bread flour
1½ tsp	osmotolerant or regular instant yeast (page 15)
1	egg white
	oil, for shaping
80 g	unsalted butter, melted, for brushing
	topping options (see pointers)

EQUIPMENT

- a stand mixer fitted with the dough hook
- two 20 or 22 cm savarin or ring moulds with rounded bases, liberally sprayed with oil-and-flour baking spray

STEP 5

STEP 6

TWO DOUGHNUTS

Blame it on my British teenhood, but to me the only real doughnut is a fat round golden one with a pale equator, a light dusting of sugar, and a core of proper jam within its bready crumb—a classic Berliner, in other words. Not for me are the coronary-inducing frosting or animal faces or bespoke custard injections. That said, my first trip to an American donut shop did leave me dazzled by the Seussian panoply of shapes and colours.

For everyone enamoured of doughnuts but leery of grease, I offer this recipe for supremely light, airy and enormous treats. It's much easier to bake big sliceable rings than to deep-fry lots of small ones—less muss, less fuss, no kitchen afug with shortening fumes, no third-degree burns because you accidentally dripped some water from your just-washed hands into the deep-fryer and made the fat splutter all over and pattern your arms with scars that last to this day. Or maybe that's just me.

METHOD

1 Make the custard. Combine all ingredients except the butter in a small pot and set over medium-low heat. Whisk constantly until mixture thickens to a gloopy consistency. Take the pot off the heat and whisk in the butter until melted and incorporated. Let cool completely.

2 Whisk flour and yeast together in a mixing bowl. Add egg white and cooled custard. Stir with a spatula to combine it all into a soft dough resembling mashed potatoes. Cover bowl with a damp tea towel and let it stand at room temperature for 30 minutes.

3 Knead the dough for 1 minute on medium speed. Re-cover bowl and let dough rest for 10 minutes. Repeat the kneading and resting once, then knead it for a final 1 to 2 minutes, until it is smooth, strongly elastic and just starts to clean the bowl sides. Scrape dough into a clean bowl lightly greased with oil, cover it, and let it stand at room temperature until risen to double its original size, about 1 hour.

4 Rub your hands and a work surface lightly with oil. Turn out the dough and press it gently all over to deflate it, then divide it in half. Roll one portion into a ball, then cup your hands around it and drag it towards you, so that it rounds and tightens in shape. Rotate the ball a quarter turn and repeat the dragging, to make it neat and spherical. Shape the other portion likewise. Let balls rest for 10 minutes.

5 Have your sprayed moulds ready. Poke an oiled finger into the centre of a ball, clear through to the work surface. Move it in widening circles to enlarge the hole, stretching the dough ring as evenly as you can, keeping its upper surface smooth. Place the dough ring in a mould. Repeat with other ball and mould. Brush doughnuts with melted butter.

6 Let them rise until only just doubled in size, about 45 minutes.

7 Preheat oven to 185°C. Place shelves in the upper and lower thirds of the oven.

8 Brush doughnuts with melted butter again. Bake for 14 minutes, then swap doughnuts between shelves and bake for 4 to 6 minutes more, until well-risen and deep golden brown. They should sound hollow when lightly tapped.

9 Unmould hot doughnuts onto a rack. Brush lightly with melted butter a final time, then let cool for a few minutes. Adorn as desired—see below—and slice to serve. Like all doughnuts, these are best eaten warm and fresh.

POINTERS

- All the butter-brushing encourages the doughnuts to rise to their fullest extent, and gives them flavoursome, burnished skins.
- For a sugar dredge: whisk equal weights of icing sugar and caster sugar together, and spike with ground spices, vanilla seeds, cocoa powder, citrus zest, ground nuts, powdered tea and such. Dredge doughnuts while they are warm.
- For a dark chocolate glaze: whisk together 15 g cocoa powder, 30 g icing sugar, 45 g water and 40 g golden syrup (or corn syrup, or honey) in a pot until smooth. Whisking constantly, bring to a simmer over medium heat. Scrape into a bowl, add 100 g finely chopped dark chocolate, and stir slowly until glaze is smooth. Pour it into a wide plate. Invert a doughnut and dip it in the glaze, then swiftly turn it right side up and place on a serving plate. Repeat with other doughnut. Yummiest while glaze and doughnut are both still warm.
- Leftovers make wonderful French toast or bread pudding.

VARIATION

- **To make two giant doughnut-ball rings:** Divide the dough into 16 equal portions. Shape each into a tight, compact round ball by cupping it under your oiled palm and dragging it in small circles on your floured work surface. Place 8 balls in a ring on a baking sheet lined with baking paper, just touching each other. Repeat with remaining balls. Brush with butter, let rise, brush again, and bake for 12 to 13 minutes.

VARIATION

- **To make two giant twist doughnuts:** Divide dough into 4 equal portions, dust them with potato starch to prevent sticking, then roll them into skinny ropes. Twist pairs of ropes together, place each twist in a greased ring mould, and pinch the ends to seal. Brush with butter, let rise, brush again, and bake for 16 to 18 minutes.

BREAD ROUX

Partially cooking flour and water together to make a paste, then adding it to bread dough during the initial mixing, is an old and traditional technique. Cooking the flour gelatinises starches and alters the crumb architecture of the final loaf, yielding a coarser, fluffier, more open texture. Furthermore, if the paste is kept within a certain temperature range, enzymes in the flour get busy converting starches into sugars, creating more depth of flavour. Bakers around the world are reviving and experimenting with this and similar methods to coax maximum flavour from different grains and flours.

Pre-gelatinised starch has a long tradition of use in Russia. Rye breads which would otherwise be lumpen and dense are rendered softer, lighter and longer-keeping with a zavarka (loosely translated as 'scald' or 'brew') mixed up from rye flour and boiling water. Other ingredients like malt or spices can be added, and zavarkas can also be fermented with yeast or lactobacilli, for even more complex flavours. German bakers similarly make brühstück ('boiling piece') with flours of wheat and other grains. In Asia, where it is called tangzhong in Mandarin and yukone in Japanese, the roux paste is often made by whisking room-temperature flour and water together, then slowly stirring it over low heat until it reaches the desired temperature and thickness.

For many breads in this book, I have used a 'custard' roux enriched with egg yolks or whole egg and fresh or powdered milk. Only after working out and refining this technique did I discover its historical precedent—a 16th-century Italian 'milk and sugar bread' recipe with hot milk and 'scalded' egg yolks. Now as then, these ingredients help make a supple dough (such as the pandan pão de deus dough shown here) that bakes up with a tender, rich-tasting crumb, and a well-coloured crust. Also, I often thicken the custard with potato starch, on which bakers have long relied to produce moist breads and cakes.

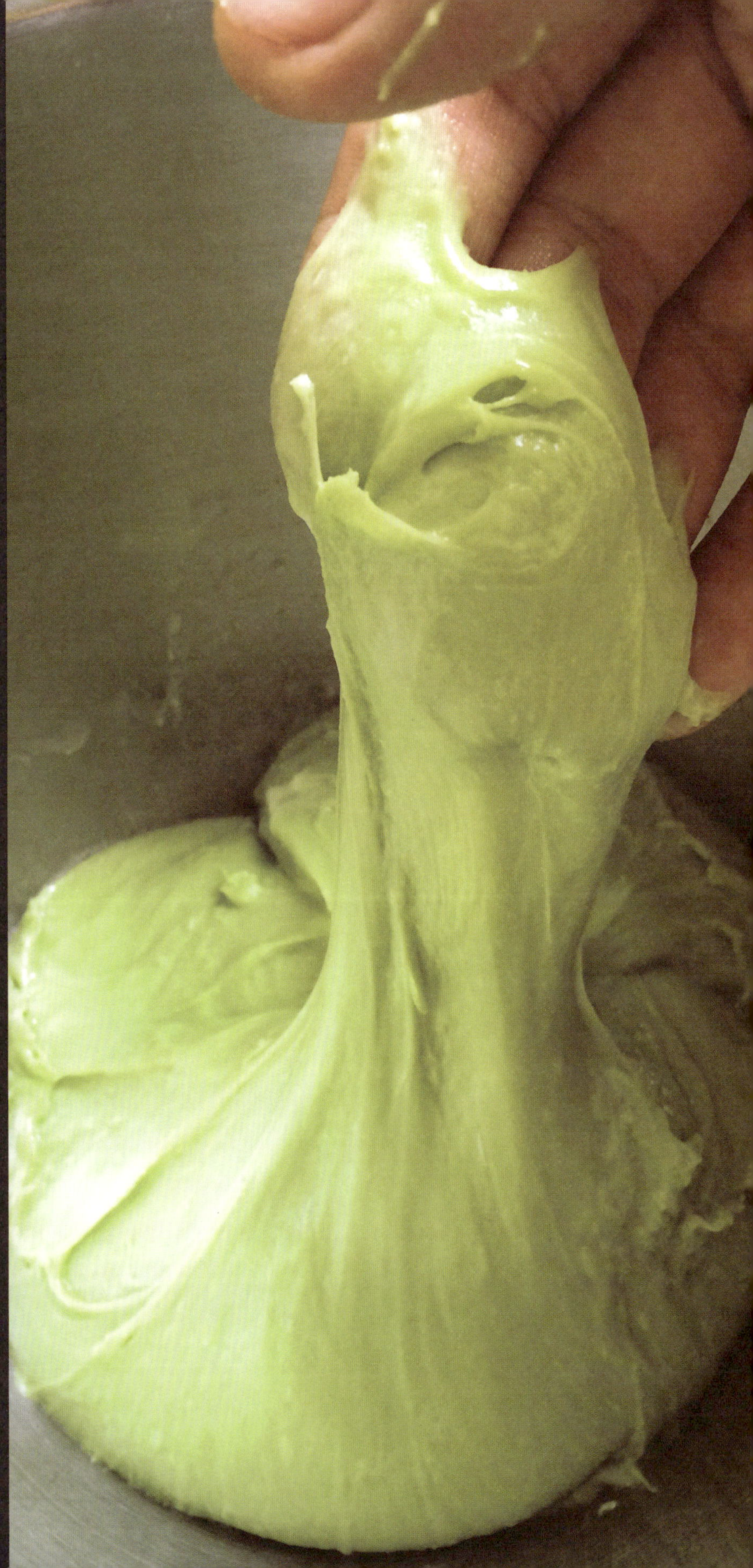

CHINA

"Oooiii!! Ni zenme le?!?"*
Visiting China keeps me moving. In Beijing I dodge breakneck bicycles, hustle down hutongs and traverse huge, broad boulevards. I hastily backpedal out of the way of autorickshaws. I traipse for miles through maze-like suburbs. I schlep up and down the Great Wall's majestic meanders.

In Hong Kong, I cruise up escalators and slip through narrow lanes. In Tibet, altitude sickness slows me to a crawl even as incredible vistas beckon me onwards. And all the while my mind leaps across distances, too, adjusting and recalibrating its understanding of Chineseness.

Is this constant motion also part of being Chinese? Perhaps. Look at how far the diaspora has been flung, how few the places lacking a Chinese restaurant. I myself am mostly Straits Chinese, a.k.a. Peranakan, a.k.a. the descendant of Chinese forebears who moved to Southeast Asia several centuries ago and married spouses whose ethnicities we cannot know at this distance. I am thereby the inheritor of cultural mores marbled by many removes from their motherland. This means that I never feel less Chinese than when I am in China, trying to find a groove.

**"Oi! What's wrong with you?!?"*

Have I mentioned that I don't speak Mandarin in any useful amount? Partly because no-one in my immediate family does either, but mostly due to primary-school Mandarin teachers who were short on both English and empathy. Eventually mastering French eased my fears of being forever second-language-blind, but it doesn't help me order lunch in (any) Chinatown. These days, I still struggle. Taxi drivers scold me. I exasperate service staff when I speak bull in a China shop.

What does all this have to do with baking, you ask? Just this: my mouth is still connected to its mother tongue. More than two days without eating rice and I perish. Heaty things give me sore throats, cooling things quench them.

I can taste a master stock and tell you pretty much what went into it. I can *almost* deshell a prawn inside my closed mouth, using only tongue and teeth. And so, in China, I feel closest to home when I bite through the crispy-crunchy-soft-pungent strata of a jianbing, the quintessential fried-eggy-breakfast-crepe. Or as I chow down on a roujiamo, the Shaanxi specialty of a chewy bun stuffed with braised pork, coriander and chillies. Or as I spoon up gongting nailao, an imperial dish of milk stirred with rice wine and slow-baked into a silken, alabaster junket.

I'm hungry now. Please excuse me while I go bake something. And also cook some rice.

Left, top to bottom: *baking buns in Tibet; Beijing duck; naizhuan, a Bejing snack of reduced-milk paste rolled with red bean paste.* ***Opposite, clockwise from top left:*** *slicing a pork ribbon for a Shanghai dish; sweet potato snack; yak butter for sale; a Lhasa view; a fennel greens bun.*

SWEET SESAME BREAD

MAKES ONE LARGE LOAF, SERVING 8 TO 12

INGREDIENTS

Dough

155 g	water
100 g	milk
1	egg
40 g	dark muscovado sugar
25 g	rye flour
¾ tsp	salt
200 g	chapati flour or wholewheat pastry flour (page 14)
185 g	bread flour, plus additional for dusting
1½ tsp	osmotolerant instant yeast (page 15)
40 g	unsalted butter, slightly softened, plus additional for greasing

Filling

130 g	dark muscovado sugar
10 g	potato starch
160 g	tahini (see pointers)
⅓ tsp	fine salt
1 tbsp	melted butter
1 tbsp	sesame seeds

EQUIPMENT

- a 2.5-litre capacity loaf tin
- a stand mixer fitted with the dough hook

STEP 7

As befits a capital city, Beijing has many Official Delicacies, conveniently arrayed at food souvenir shops or local snack cafes. At one of the latter I sampled tang huoshao, a dusky square cobblestone of a bun. Its coarse, soft brown crumb was a tad dry, but rippled through it were veins of sesame paste and brown sugar that mandated another bite, and another, until it was gone. I've recaptured the spirit of that little bread in loaf form, with a bit of added butter for a more moist texture not unlike a European babka. The flavours of wholewheat flour and rye flour compliment the sesame very well.

METHOD

1 Combine water, milk, egg, muscovado sugar, rye flour and salt in a small pot. Set over medium-low heat and cook, whisking constantly, until mixture thickens into a creamy custard. Scrape into a bowl and let cool completely; it will continue to thicken as it cools.

2 Whisk chapati flour, bread flour and yeast together in a mixing bowl. Add custard and stir with a spatula until a stiff, shaggy dough forms. Cover bowl with a damp tea towel and let it stand for 20 minutes.

3 Knead the dough on medium-low speed for 1 minute. Re-cover bowl and let dough rest for 5 minutes. Repeat the kneading and resting once more. Finally, add butter and knead until it is incorporated and dough has come back together into a slightly sticky, slightly springy ball— it will not be as elastic as regular white bread dough.

4 Turn the dough out onto a lightly floured work surface. Divide it in half and shape each portion into a round ball. Let the balls rest for a few minutes while you make the filling.

5 To make the filling, push muscovado sugar and potato starch through a sieve into a bowl, to get out any lumps. Stir in tahini and salt until well blended.

6 Roll out a dough ball into a square roughly 35 cm across. Rotate the dough between every few strokes, and roll slowly so that it extends without tearing. This is a fairly slack dough that should not resist or snap back too much. Dollop half the filling on top, and spread it very thinly and evenly across the dough. Starting at the edge nearest you, roll up the dough tightly into a cylinder, and pinch seams and ends to seal. Repeat the above with the remaining dough and filling.

7 Grease loaf tin well with butter. Twist the two dough cylinders together to make a tight double helix, and place in the loaf tin. Cover with greased plastic wrap. Let rise at cool room temperature until just doubled in size, about 50 minutes.

8 Preheat oven to 190°C at least 10 minutes before the bread is ready to bake. Place a shelf in the middle position.

9 Brush risen loaf gently with melted butter and sprinkle with sesame seeds. Bake for 30 to 35 minutes, until deeply browned and it sounds hollow when lightly

tapped. It may not rise very much. To double-check if it's done, stick a cake tester or skewer into the loaf's middle—it should emerge damp, but without any raw dough sticking to it.

10 Transfer loaf tin to a rack. Let cool for at least 20 minutes before serving. Leftovers will keep, tightly wrapped and chilled, for 2 to 3 days. Re-warm to serve.

POINTERS

- Chinese brands of roasted sesame seed paste will work for this recipe, but those I've tasted have had bitter or burnt notes more often than not. Hence I usually use a mellow, taupe-coloured roasted sesame seed tahini from the Middle East. Raw tahini tastes too...well, raw. For a dramatic visual contrast between filling and crumb, use unsweetened Japanese black sesame seed paste.
- Tang huoshao are often flavoured with osmanthus, tiny yellow flowers scented like peaches and honeysuckle. I'm not a great fan of them. If you are, steep 1 tbsp dried osmanthus in 2 tbsp hot water for 10 minutes, then strain and add the liquid to the filling, along with an extra ½ tsp potato starch.
- Serve this loaf warm for breakfast or brunch, with cheeses and fruit. Slices of baked or cured ham wouldn't go amiss either.

MAKES ONE LARGE BREAD, SERVING 3 TO 6

INGREDIENTS

290 g	plain flour
1 tsp	instant yeast (page 15)
150 g	boiled and cooled water
50 g	chapati flour (page 14)
40 g	sugar
¾ tsp	salt
50 g	salted butter
75 g	plain unsweetened yoghurt
½ tsp	saffron threads
4 tbsp	warm milk

EQUIPMENT

- a stand mixer fitted with the dough hook, or elbow grease
- a baking sheet
- baking paper
- a dough scraper or large blunt knife

POINTERS

- Serve this plain with honey, butter or cheese, or with braised dishes that have plenty of gravy to sop up. It would go perfectly with chicken kurmah (page 195).

A FISTFUL OF FLATBREAD

As I wandered around Lhasa's narrow lanes, a bakery made me stop. Not just because of the wide, puffy breads on display, but because Clint Eastwood was behind the counter. Or rather, his Tibetan baker doppelganger. Hamstrung by my non-command of Mandarin, I took away from our encounter only smiles, photos and a flatbread. Grid-grooved, with a faint wash of something yellow and speckles of char, it was good, honest bread, decently chewy, slightly sweet, spongy enough to soak up sauce but flavourful enough to eat plain.

This recipe is not an exact replica—it couldn't be, without the essential ingredients of Lhasa evening light, the cool air, and the beaming faces of Clint and family. Having sipped lovely saffron tea at a medical hall in Tibet, I chose to brush my bread with saffron milk wash, which gives it a likeness to a sheermal, a classic bread of Lucknow and Hyderabad. As those cities' cuisines do boast Central Asian influences, the resemblance might in fact be quite appropriate.

METHOD

1 Whisk 40 g of the plain flour, yeast and water together in a bowl until smooth. Cover and let stand at room temperature for 30 minutes, until slightly bubbly.

2 Combine the remaining 250 g plain flour, chapati flour, sugar and salt in a mixing bowl, and whisk to blend. Add butter and rub it in with your fingertips until it disperses and mixture resembles fine sand. Add yeast mixture and yoghurt to the bowl, and mix with a spatula until a rough dough forms. Cover bowl with a damp tea towel and let dough rest for 20 minutes.

3 Knead the dough for 2 minutes on low speed, then re-cover bowl and let dough rest for 5 minutes. (If kneading by hand, use the stretch-fold technique—see page 30.) Knead for another 2 minutes on

low speed, until dough has become more smooth and is slightly springy. It will not be as elastic as regular white bread dough. Re-cover bowl and let dough rise until doubled in size, about 1 hour.

4 Place a sheet of baking paper on your work surface and dust it lightly with flour. Turn out dough onto paper and gently deflate it with your hands. Working slowly and smoothly so the dough extends without snapping back, roll it out into a round about 1 cm thick and about 35 cm in diameter. Lift it up now and then as you roll, so that it doesn't stick to the paper and the paper doesn't buckle. Slide paper and dough together onto the baking sheet. Let it rise in your turned-off oven until puffy and barely doubled in size, about 45 to 55 minutes.

5 About 15 minutes before the dough is ready, combine the saffron and warm milk in a small bowl and set aside, covered.

6 Remove the bread from the oven. Preheat oven to 190°C. Place a shelf in the lower third of the oven.

7 Brush the dough all over with the saffron milk. With the edge of the dough scraper, gently press parallel lines into the dough, spaced about 2 cm apart. Press deeply but do not sever the dough into strips. Press another set of parallel lines perpendicular to the first, to end up with a grid pattern. Brush the dough all over again with the saffron milk.

8 Bake bread for 20 to 25 minutes, until risen and golden on top, and pale gold underneath. Do not over-bake or bread will be dry.

9 Transfer baking sheet to a rack and let bread cool. Serve warm or at room temperature.

FRANCE

I needed 15 minutes of pacing and angst-ridden rehearsal to mutter my first French words ever to a French person: "*Une gaufre au chocolat, s'il vous plaît.*"

I was on a school history trip to World War II sites in Northern France, with a bunch of fellow students baying to get tanked on cheap Orangina and a bunch of teachers equally eager for stronger bottled stuff. It was *incroyable*, all of it: getting lost in a cavernous *hypermarché*; climbing around a crumbling war bunker on a deserted beach; tasting gross French boarding house seaweed soup; goggling at the Bayeux Tapestry, 900 years old but looking fresh from a craftsman's hands; on another beach, bumping (not literally) into the boarding house waitress sunbathing topless. (We asked her to pose with our rotund, pink-faced form teacher Mr CJ for a photo, and she obliged with sunny insouciance.)

Three other things I cannot forget. Feeling something numinous brush my mind amid Bayeux Cathedral's shafts of light and stone. The sight of the Normandy American Cemetery's sweeping, numberless white crosses hammering home the fact of the war in a way that the classroom never could. And, after two semesters of lip-twisting *leçons*, forcing myself to *parler français* for the reward of a chocolate-sauced gaufre, or waffle. Like my French, it was under-cooked and far from perfect, but came garnished with a glow of triumph.

Left: *Autumn in a Parisian park.*

Things escalated from there. My French reached conversational level, and more importantly, cookbook level. I watched chefs Michel and Albert Roux bake a golden Gateau Pithiviers at a showcase—a seminal moment on my own journey to bakerhood. I learnt to love raw-milk cheeses. I sipped cognac in Cognac, where an auberge cat brought me a mouse for breakfast.

And as I grew to love French food, it changed how I cook. In 2010, I accompanied a contingent from the Singapore Peranakan Association to Paris, to conduct cultural activities alongside an exhibition of artifacts loaned from Singapore's Peranakan Museum to the Musée Quai Branly.

For my cooking demos, I took the chance to reframe flavours from my heritage *à la française*. Peranakan nasi ulam, an aromatic herbed salad, I made with couscous instead of rice. Pineapple tarts and sago pudding I combined, de- and re-constructing them as a verrine (dessert in a glass) of tapioca pearls bathed in creamy coconut, topped with caramelised and spiced sautéed pineapple. The Parisian visitors finished every crumb.

Et enfin, to visit me at the exhibition came a French pen-friend. I'd connected with food expert and cookbook author Marie-Claire Frédéric months before via her blog, *Du Miel et Du Sel*, and we'd kept in touch ever since. Via her Singapore-based daughter and online translators, we traded thoughts and recipes, illuminating our respective gastronomic worlds for each other. Seeing her at last in person, I felt the circle close.

Here I was once again, speaking about food in French with a French person, only this time without angst, and the sure promise of *bien manger*.

Left, top to bottom: *I love cheese; a cellar in Cognac; mouse for breakfast.* ***Opposite, clockwise from top left:*** *a vineyard in the south; cooking at the MQB; wild mushrooms; baked custards; at the Salon du Chocolat.*

Oeuf au lait
€ 1,65
la barquette

CHOCOLATE MATCHA MACARON TART

In 2010, I attended Paris' annual Salon du Chocolat, a celebration of all things cacao, with exhibitions, cooking demos, cultural performances and, most crucially, retail. The convention-centre venue heaved with chocolate made into confections, cakes, pastries and ice creams, blocks and truffles and gigantic teddy bears, and—this being Paris—haute couture garments. Totally, wonderfully head-spinning. One of the longest queues was for pâtissier Sadaharu Aoki's imagawayaki. In Japan, these drum-shaped pancakes usually enclose red bean paste in plain batter, but the Parisians were lining up for matcha pancakes, *each stuffed with a large whole chocolate macaron*. Imagine: soft, almost custardy cake with green tea's bitter and umami notes, giving way to the dark macaron's more ardent bittersweetness, its heart of rich chocolate ganache slightly cool next to the warm, steamy cake. *Quelle extase!* Here, I have recast those flavours in a classic tarte au chocolat topped with matcha-pistachio macaron batter.

SERVES 10 TO 16

INGREDIENTS

Pastry

200 g	plain flour
70 g	icing sugar
10 g	cornstarch
¼ tsp	fine salt
110 g	very cold unsalted butter, diced
1	egg

Chocolate layer

120 g	dark chocolate (see pointers)
100 g	whipping cream
50 g	milk
35 g	caster sugar
⅛ tsp	salt
¼ tsp	vanilla extract
2	egg yolks

Matcha macaron layer

80 g	shelled pistachio nuts
90 g	icing sugar
10 g	matcha powder, sifted
2	egg whites
50 g	caster sugar
	icing sugar, for dusting

EQUIPMENT

- a loose-bottomed 23 cm square (or 25 cm round) tart pan, with sides at least 2 cm high
- a food processor

POINTERS

- Use chocolate with around 65 to 70 per cent cacao—a higher percentage might overshadow the flavour of the matcha.
- I make this with regular pistachios still bearing fragments of their skins, as I find that blanching them so you can rub their skins off mutes their already subtle flavour. If you can get skinned shelled pistachios, by all means use those.

METHOD

1 Make the pastry. Sift flour, icing sugar and cornstarch into a mixing bowl. Whisk in salt. Add butter and rub it in with your fingertips, until it disperses and mixture looks like fine sand. Beat egg and add to bowl, and stir until dough forms a ball. Knead very briefly to even it out, then wrap dough in plastic wrap and chill for 1 hour.

2 Sandwich the dough between 2 sheets of baking paper. Roll it out to about 3 mm thick. Peel off top paper sheet. Lift up the pastry on the bottom sheet and invert it over the tart tin, centring it as best you can. Peel off the paper. Without stretching it, press the pastry evenly over the pan base and 2.5 cm up its sides. Trim off and save any excess pastry. Replace the paper and gently press it flush against the pastry shell all around. Freeze the shell for 1 hour, or chill it for at least 8 hours.

3 Preheat oven to 190°C. Place a shelf in the middle position. Measure and set out all ingredients for the chocolate and macaron layers.

4 Peel paper off pastry. Bake the tart shell for 15 minutes, until just barely done. Remove shell from oven. *Turn oven down to 160°C.*

5 If the shell has any cracks or holes, patch them by smearing and pressing blobs of the saved pastry into them. Let it stand while you make the chocolate layer.

6 Make the chocolate layer. Place chocolate in a heatproof bowl and set aside. Combine cream, milk, sugar and salt in a saucepan. Bring up to a simmer over medium heat, whisking frequently, then pour over chocolate. Let it stand for 30 seconds, then stir mixture with a whisk until smooth. Whisk in vanilla and egg yolks until smooth.

7 Pour the filling into the warm pastry shell. Return it to the oven and bake for 8 minutes.

8 Make the macaron batter. Pulse-blend pistachio nuts and icing sugar together in a food processor until nuts are very finely and uniformly ground—do not overdo it, or they will turn into an oily paste. Whisk in matcha.

9 In a clean, grease-free bowl, beat egg whites until soft peaks form, then add caster sugar and beat until stiff, glossy peaks form. Fold in half of the pistachio mixture with a spatula until it is barely mixed in, then add remaining mixture and fold in until incorporated, about 10 to 12 sweeps of the spatula. Stop folding when the batter has thinned out enough to slowly slough off the spatula in a glossy ribbon—when it falls back into the bowl, the ribbon should take several seconds to disappear back into the batter.

10 Note: *if the chocolate layer is ready before the macaron batter is finished, remove the tart from the oven and let it stand in the meantime.*

11 Remove tart from oven. Turn oven temperature up to 170°C. Gently spread macaron batter evenly over chocolate layer. Burst any bubbles that appear with the tip of a skewer. Return tart shell to oven. Bake for 16 minutes.

12 Transfer tart pan to a rack and let it cool completely. The filling will sink slightly as it cools. Chill it for 20 minutes before serving.

13 Before serving, dust with icing sugar, with or without a stencil as you please. Slice with a very sharp knife, wiping it with a clean damp cloth or paper towel between cuts.

Sadaharu Aoki's original macaron yaki.

CHOUX TOURTEAUX

I originally wanted to give you a recipe for tourteau fromager (pictured below). I'd seen this blackly inscrutable, tarmac-domed specialty at a market in Cognac—surely not food? Slicing it revealed a light and airy cheesecake under the charred top, barely sweet, with the lilt of fresh goat cheese and not a hint of singe. Fortunately, my friend Marie-Claire hails from Poitou-Charentes, tourteau fromager's birthplace, and she sent me baking pans, a detailed recipe and priceless advice. The very first time I made it, it came out almost perfect; but every subsequent trial was a dud, with cracks or other flaws. Weeks of testing brought me no nearer consistent results. I surmised that the cake is sensitive to even slight variations in goat cheeses and ovens, which both may differ just too much between Singapore and France. So here instead are my tributes to tourteau fromager, inspired by my friendship with Marie-Claire. Their shells ('tourteau' means crab) are authentically black, but from sesame seeds instead of a very-high-heat bake.

MAKES 20 CHOUX PUFFS

INGREDIENTS

Black sesame craquelin

30 g	black sesame seeds
40 g	plain flour
50 g	light brown sugar
50 g	unsalted butter, diced and slightly softened

Goat cheese mousse filling

325 g	fresh young goat cheese
130 g	icing sugar, sifted
1 tbsp	cognac
275 g	whipping cream

Choux pastry

100 g	plain flour
25 g	bread flour
110 g	water
100 g	milk
85 g	unsalted butter
1 tsp	sesame oil
1 tsp	sugar
½ tsp	salt
2	egg whites, at room temperature
3	eggs, at room temperature

EQUIPMENT

- a blender or food processor
- baking sheets lined with baking paper
- piping bags and round and star piping tips
- patience
- a small round cookie cutter

METHOD

1 Make black sesame craquelin ('crah-ker-lahn'). Combine all ingredients except butter in a blender or food processor and pulse-blend until seeds are finely ground. Transfer mixture to a bowl. Add butter and work it in with a spatula to make a smooth paste. Sandwich the paste between two sheets of baking paper, and roll it out to 2 mm thickness. Freeze it until firm, at least 30 minutes.

2 Make the filling. Push goat cheese through a sieve to remove any lumps, then fold in icing sugar and cognac with a spatula until smoothly. In another bowl, whip the cream until stiff peaks just start to form. Gently whisk a third of the whipped cream into the cheese mixture, then fold in the remaining whipped cream in 2 additions. Scrape mousse into a piping bag fitted with a small plain or star tip, twist to seal, and chill until needed.

3 Make choux pastry dough. Sift both flours into a bowl, whisk very well to mix, and set aside. Combine water, milk, butter, sesame oil, sugar and salt in a heavy saucepan, cover tightly and bring to a full boil over medium heat. Uncover pan and add flour mixture all at once. Immediately take the pan off the heat and beat with a heatproof spatula or wooden spoon until dough forms a ball. Reduce heat to medium-low, place the pan back over it, and beat the dough slowly and steadily for about 3 minutes, so that it dries out slightly. Scrape dough into a bowl and let it cool until very warm to the touch.

4 With a spatula by hand, or a mixer paddle attachment, beat both egg whites into the dough until incorporated. Beat in 1 egg until incorporated, then a second egg. Finally, beat the last egg with a fork in a small bowl to blend it, then beat it into the dough *a couple of teaspoons at a time*. You may not use it all—*stop adding egg* when the dough is glossy, smooth and thick enough that, if you stick a wet fingertip about 1 cm into the dough and drag it along, the trough it leaves behind holds its shape and does not collapse in on itself. If you drop some dough onto a flat surface, it should only sag a tad; if it spreads into a flat puddle, too much egg has been added, and there is no returning from that. Scrape the dough into a piping bag fitted with a plain round tip.

5 Preheat oven to 200°C. Place a shelf in the lower third of the oven.

6 Holding the bag vertically, pipe round choux about 4 cm in diameter on a paper-lined baking sheet, spacing them about 5 cm apart. Dip your fingertips in a bowl of water and sprinkle droplets all over the baking sheet—this will boost oven humidity and choux puffage.

7 Remove the craquelin from freezer. Peel off top sheet of paper. With a round or fluted cutter, stamp out discs 4 cm in diameter. Lift out the rounds with a palette knife or butter knife, and place one round on each piped chou. Work swiftly, as the topping softens fast.

8 Bake the choux for 15 to 17 minutes, until they have just stopped expanding—they will first spread out laterally, then subsequently puff upward and out—and the fissures in the craquelin are beginning to brown. Reduce the heat to 175°C (without opening the oven door) and bake for 15 to 20 minutes more, until choux are crisp and dark black-brown.

9 Transfer baking sheet to a rack. Let the choux cool down slowly, away from drafts, so that they keep their shape.

10 Poke a hole in the bottom of a cooled chou with a chopstick tip. Insert the tip of the piping bag of mousse, and squeeze gently until the chou feels full. Fill remaining choux likewise. Serve immediately.

POINTERS

- For the most even rise, bake only one tray of choux at a time.
- In my humid apartment, the crisp tops of the baked choux start to soften within an hour of being baked. Fill them and serve them as soon as they have cooled to enjoy the maximum contrast of all the textures. Otherwise, stash the cooled choux in a very airtight container until needed.

STEP 7

MAKES 8 KOUIGNOU-AMANN

INGREDIENTS

150 g	plain flour, plus additional for dusting
100 g	bread flour
1 tsp	fine salt
190 g	cold, firm unsalted butter (see pointers), plus additional for greasing
145 g	boiled and cooled water
2 tsp	osmotolerant or regular instant yeast (page 15)
1½ tbsp	plain flour
220 g	fine sugar
10 to 12 slices	streaky bacon
large pinch	black pepper

EQUIPMENT

- a small metal tray to hold the raw dough
- 8 muffin tins or foil cups, about 10 cm in diameter and at least 2 cm deep
- a baking tray large enough to hold the cups spaced about 3 cm apart
- patience

BACON KOUIGNOU-AMANN

Specialties of Brittany (singular: kouign-amann, pronounced 'kween-ah-mahnn'), these are made with a lean yeasted dough, laminated with lots of butter just like puff pastry—but also with ample sugar. As they bake, the sugar traps moisture, melts and caramelises where it seeps out, making puffy internal layers and gorgeously crispy outer ones. I am too ashamed to confess how many kouignou-amann I gobbled during four days in Paris—suffice to say, enough to make me vow to learn how to bake them. And also to sign up for a gym membership.*

I can't easily essay classic puff or Danish pastry in my sweltering kitchen. However, I do make rough puff pastry, where all the cubed butter is mixed into the dough at the outset, instead of being layered in. Could I adapt this method to kouignou-amann? *Beh oui!* And also, mmmm, bacon.

**I haven't.*

METHOD

1 Whisk 150 g plain flour, bread flour and salt together in a bowl until well mixed. Cut the butter into 5 mm-thick slabs, then slice those into 2.5 cm-wide pieces, and toss them with the flour to mix well. Cover bowl tightly and freeze for 2 hours (or chill overnight), until flour and butter are both very cold.

2 Whisk water, yeast and the 1½ tablespoons of plain flour together in a small bowl. Let stand at room temperature for 20 to 30 minutes, until a little bubbly.

3 Take the flour and butter out of the fridge. Stir the yeast mixture, scrape all of it into the bowl, then stir with a spatula until the dough comes together in a shaggy ball. Resist the temptation to add more water—if the dough is too moist it will be trickier to roll later. Press the dough and any dry bits together, wrap in plastic wrap, flatten into a slab, place on a metal tray and chill for at least 1 hour, until firm.

4 Place a large sheet of baking paper on your counter and dust it lightly but evenly with flour. Unwrap dough, place on paper, and dust its top lightly with flour. Roll out into a thin sheet about 30 cm by 40 cm. The dough will resemble terrazzo flooring, spangled with embedded butter (see photo overleaf). Fold the lower third of the sheet up to cover its central third, then fold its top third down likewise, as you would fold a business letter. You now have a dough oblong with 3 layers.

5 Rotate the dough 90 degrees, flatten it slightly with the rolling pin, and repeat the folding. If needed along the way, dust with a bit more flour to prevent the butter smearing, but be sparing. You now have a chubby dough block with 9 layers. Wrap it up in the baking paper, place on the tray, and chill for 1 hour to 90 minutes, until firm.

(continued on the next page)

6 Unwrap the dough but leave it on the baking paper. Dust lightly all over with flour again, then roll it out into a 30 cm by 40 cm sheet. Fold the bottom third up and top third down as before. Your dough block now has 27 layers. Rewrap dough and chill for 1 hour.

7 Grease the muffin tins or foil cups well with butter and space them out on a baking tray.

8 Unwrap the dough. Sprinkle 80 g of the sugar over the dough, then turn it upside down. Sprinkle 80 g more sugar over the dough. Using the rolling pin to press the sugar into it, roll the dough into a rectangle about 25 cm by 40 cm.

9 Lay the bacon strips over the dough, parallel to its shorter side and spaced slightly apart. Sprinkle 40 g more sugar and the black pepper over the bacon. Starting from a shorter side, roll up the dough tightly like a Swiss roll, forming a compact log. No need to pinch the seam—the kouignou-amann need to expand outward as they rise.

10 With a sharp knife, cut log into 8 slices. Place a slice in each tin or cup. Space cups 3 cm apart on a baking tray. Cover loosely with greased plastic wrap. Let stand at cool room temperature for 1 hour, until slightly puffy. They might bleed some liquid—this is fine.

11 Preheat oven to 200°C. Place a shelf in the middle position.

12 Sprinkle the remaining 20 g sugar over the kouignou-amann. Bake for 3 minutes, then turn the oven temperature down to 180°C and bake for 30 to 32 minutes more, until risen and deeply caramelised.

13 Remove the kouignou-amann from the oven. Let them stand for 2 minutes for any caramel bubbles to subside, then immediately remove them from their tins and place them on a rack or baking-paper lined tray. Do not wait longer than this, or the caramelised sugar will set hard and it will be nearly impossible to pry them loose.

14 Devour the kouignou-amann while warm. Sigh contentedly.

POINTERS

- Kouignou-amann are traditionally made with salted butter, but I find that a little overkill with the salty bacon, so I use unsalted butter. If you prefer to use salted butter, reduce the fine salt by half. In either case, opt for a French or European butter with a high fat content, at least 82 per cent.
- The best quality flour, butter and bacon make all the difference.
- Be as precise as you can when cutting up the cold butter, as this makes the lamination more even.
- It is crucial to keep the dough cold during the rolling and folding, as the lamination will be messy if the butter softens too much. If your kitchen is warm and the dough softens too quickly at any point, cover it and return it to the fridge to firm up before proceeding. On a hot day I chill it for 90 minutes before each rolling and folding session.

PSEUDO CROISSANTS

Before you ask: yes, you can make croissant-ish rolls from this dough—they will taste good, but won't be as light and airy as proper croissants, which require much more precise lamination for their signature texture. Apply these alterations, then, for pseudo croissants:

- In step 1, add 2 tablespoons of caster sugar to the flour mixture, and increase the amount of salt to 1¼ teaspoons.
- In step 4, instead of a three-ply letter fold, make a four-ply book fold—fold opposite ends of the rectangle to its midline, then fold all in half. Steps 5 and 6 remain three-ply folds.
- In step 8, omit the sugar. Roll the dough into a rectangle 20 cm wide by 40 cm long. With a sharp knife, cut it into 4 smaller rectangles, 10 cm wide by 20 cm long, then halve each rectangle along a diagonal. Gently roll out the short corner of a dough triangle to extend it, making the triangle isosceles and symmetrical, then roll it up tightly, from its shortest side to its point. Place it on a baking sheet, leaving it straight or curving it, as you like. Make all pseudo croissants likewise, and space them at least 4 cm apart on the baking sheet.
- Let pseudo croissants proof at cool room temperature for 70 to 90 minutes, until puffy but not quite doubled in size.
- Bake them in a preheated oven at 200°C for 10 minutes, then turn oven down to 175°C and bake for 10 to 15 minutes more, until deeply browned.

THE PHILIPPINES

There are always at least three lively, loud conversations going on simultaneously at our Filipino food gang meetings. Politics, history, art, gardening, hometown news, current events and on-going obsessions, ecology...and sometimes we even talk about food.

I'm kidding. We *always* talk about food. And we always eat well. Our motley crew of Filipino expats, Filipino-Singaporeans and one omnivorous Singaporean (me) first met years ago over a project to help needy students via a fundraising cookbook, whose photoshoots required much discussion and recipe testing. The shoots ended but the meals and chats didn't. Both continually strengthen my belief that Filipino food is underappreciated as one of the world's great creole cuisines, and one of its most diverse and vital, period. Its mix of native, Chinese, Iberian, American and other influences, fed by the nation's wide spectrum of climates and coastlines, is spectacularly, fearlessly polysyllabic. Once, over two days in Manila, I ate: a steamed siopao bun as big as an infant's head, stuffed with pork, chicken, salted egg and vegetables; tsokolate-eh, gloriously thick hot chocolate with a longer finish than most movie credits; lato, grapey seaweed which pops in the mouth like tiny balloons; a garlicky relish of taba ng talangka, unctuous orange crab roe fragrant as Davy Jones'

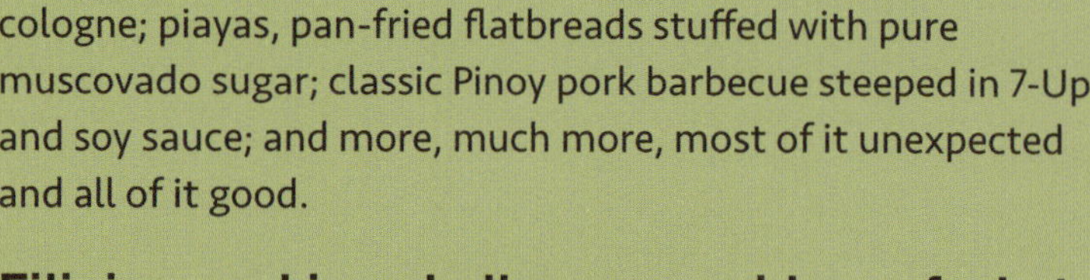

cologne; piayas, pan-fried flatbreads stuffed with pure muscovado sugar; classic Pinoy pork barbecue steeped in 7-Up and soy sauce; and more, much more, most of it unexpected and all of it good.

Filipino cooking challenges my ideas of what flavours might play well together and how one might coax them to. Oxtail stewed until nearly molten with annatto seed oil, shrimp paste, peanut butter, eggplant and snake beans? Delicious.

Fried fish served with a dip of rice fermented into a creamy, lactic paste? Perfectly logical partners. A coconut-rich sticky rice and chicken paella, cooked in a banana-leaf-lined pan until the rice—but, magically, not the leaf—is browned and crusty? I'm having thirds. Forget the screechy instant mixes tragically abundant at most Pinoy grocery shops. Getting to know real Filipino food is like walking towards an Impressionist painting: washes of flavour resolve into a hundred fine gradations of salty, sour, syrupy, starchy.

Pinoy baking traditions combine legacies and ingredients of New and Old Worlds with unique flair. I've tried to capture it in these recipes, which were queried, tasted, chewed over and approval-stamped by my gang before making the cut for this book.

Left, top to bottom: *suman sa ibos, sticky rice wrapped in palm leaves; lato seaweed salad; another suman with purple rice and millet.* ***Opposite, clockwise from top left:*** *grinding cacao; pork crackling; Casa Manila in Manila's Intramuros district; paper rolls of cacao tablea discs for making hot chocolate; cheesy mussels.*

Jemherlyn's CHICHARON
Bituka Bulaklak
CHICHARON BITUKA
50grms. P30.00
100grms. P60.00
1/4kl. P150.00
1/2kl. P300.00
1kl. P600.00

SPECIAL
SWEETENED
CHOCOLATE
₱50.00

DURIAN AND COFFEE LECHE FLAN CAKE

A thoroughly Pinoy flavour combination, showcased in a classic American cake baked together with a layer of Spanish custard flan.

Mindanao is a major coffee-growing region of the Philippines, and its southern Davao provinces are also known for durian. Some years ago, enterprising Davao City cafe owners began adding durian puree to coffee beverages, with smashing success. The flavour profiles of durian and coffee do in fact overlap. Besides the sulphurous garlicky and oniony notes which send some wussy eaters lunging for the rudest epithets in their thesauri, durian contains aroma compounds that smell of apple, rum, brandy, burnt sugar, cocoa and yes, coffee. In my own durian tastings—ok, ok, binges—I've picked up hints of almond, hazelnut, butter, sherry, banana and vanilla in different cultivars. The bittersweet nuances which many durian connoisseurs prize can entwine quite harmoniously with the bitterness of coffee. All of which is to say—make this cake, you won't regret it.

SERVES 8 TO 12

INGREDIENTS

Caramel

130 g	sugar
3 tbsp	water

Flan

225 g	durian flesh
180 g	condensed milk
20 g	raw sugar, or regular white sugar
130 g	fresh milk
3	egg yolks
2	whole eggs
½ tsp	vanilla extract, preferably Tahitian

Cake batter

115 g	cake flour, sifted
1¼ tsp	baking powder
1 tbsp	instant espresso powder or instant coffee granules
45 g	warm water
1 tbsp	plain unsweetened yoghurt
65 g	light muscovado sugar
55 g	vegetable oil
3	egg yolks
¼ tsp	coffee extract (optional)
¼ tsp	salt
3	egg whites
⅓ tsp	cream of tartar
70 g	caster sugar

EQUIPMENT

- a blender or food processor
- a one-piece round cake pan, 21 cm in diameter and at least 8 cm deep, washed and dried
- a roasting tray or baking pan big enough to hold the cake pan with at least 3 cm clearance all round
- boiling water, for a water bath

METHOD

1 Preheat oven to 175°C. Place a shelf in the middle position. Get all your equipment ready. Measure out every ingredient in readiness.

2 Make the caramel. Pour the sugar into a heavy-based metal pot. Pour the water over the centre of the sugar. Set over medium-high heat. Gently swirl the pot as the sugar melts. It may recrystallise slightly as the water evaporates—wait for it to liquefy, and watch it closely as it starts to colour. As soon as the caramel turns a deep, foxy amber, take the pot off the heat and pour its contents into the cake pan, tilting the pan so the caramel coats its base evenly. It will harden rapidly. Set pan aside.

3 Make the flan mixture. Whizz durian flesh, condensed milk and raw sugar together in a blender until smooth. Scrape mixture into a bowl, add remaining flan ingredients and stir with a whisk until smoothly blended. Do not beat—you don't want to whip any air into it. Strain mixture through a sieve. Set aside.

4 Make the chiffon cake batter. Sift cake flour and baking powder into a bowl and whisk to blend. In a mixing bowl, dissolve espresso powder in the warm water, then beat in yoghurt, muscovado, oil, egg yolks, coffee extract and salt until smooth. Add cake flour and whisk until smooth. Set aside momentarily. In a clean, grease-free bowl, beat egg whites with cream of tartar until soft peaks form, then gradually beat in caster sugar. Beat until stiff, glossy, snow-white peaks just start to form—do not over-beat. Fold the meringue into the coffee batter in 3 additions, scraping the bowl base and sides as you fold to ensure thorough mixing.

5 Give the flan mixture a final good stir, then gently pour it into the caramel-lined pan. Gently ladle the chiffon cake batter over the flan mixture. Place the pan inside the roasting tray, place the tray on the oven shelf, then fill the tray with boiling water to come at least 3 cm up the side of the cake pan.

6 Bake for 45 to 55 minutes. A thin cake tester or skewer inserted into the cake's middle, all the way through both layers, should emerge damp but without any raw flan or cake batter clinging to it.

7 Carefully lift cake tin out of the water bath and transfer it to a rack to cool. It will deflate a little as it does so. Cover completely cooled cake with plastic wrap, then chill it for at least 4 hours. The wait is essential for the caramel layer to absorb water from the flan, simultaneously firming up the flan and liquefying itself into a sauce.

8 To unmould the cake, run a thin-bladed knife around its edge, and invert a rimmed serving plate on top. Holding plate and cake pan tightly together, reinvert both. The cake should slide out. (Doing this in front of your guests runs the risk of humiliating accident or thunderous applause. Just so you know.) Lift off the cake pan. Slice to serve.

POINTERS

- Save your most expensive durians for eating neat; just make sure the fruit that you use for this cake is decently fragrant, with a little bittersweetness.
- Experimenting with vanilla once led me to discover that Tahitian vanilla extract's bright, cherry-like character subtly boosts the floral qualities of durian over its oniony side.
- Once you start making this cake, work smoothly through until it goes into the oven, without delay or breaking off to do something else.
- This cake may take up to 1 hour to bake until it tests done, depending on the exact size of your water bath and the heat circulation in your oven.

MAKES ONE RICH TART, SERVING 8 TO 12

INGREDIENTS

Crust

90 g	plain flour
90 g	cake flour
¼ tsp	salt
85 g	cold unsalted butter, diced
80 g	mature cheddar cheese
2 tbsp	ice-cold water

Filling

330 g	coconut water (see pointers)
130 g	caster sugar
20 g	cornstarch
20 g	water chestnut starch (see pointers)
85 g	coconut cream
1¼ cups	coconut flesh, cut into small pieces or strands
¼ tsp	salt
1½ tbsp	unsalted butter, cut into small bits

EQUIPMENT

- a 20 cm round springform tin, or loose-bottomed tart pan

POINTERS

- Coarse and granular water chestnut starch gives the tart filling a soft but faintly resilient gelled set. Look for it at Asian or Chinese grocery shops, packed in cardboard boxes. If you can't find it, substitute wheat starch, or more cornstarch, though the filling will be a bit softer.

BUKO COCONUT AND CHEDDAR TART

One thing about Filipino cooking that I find quirkily charming is how cheese can pop up almost anywhere, often played off against sweet or sour flavours. I have a compilation of winning recipes from a nationwide Filipino cooking competition in the 1980s, and cheese appears in nearly half of them. Not just in a Corned Beef Bake, a Pork Luncheon Meat Foldover and a Wonka-worthy casserole with 50 ingredients (including nine different meats), but also in a chocolate and candied bilimbi (sour starfruit) chiffon cake, and a Rainbow Surprise Cake with fruit cocktail and coconut. In the same spirit of invention, I've turned classic Filipino buko pie—a two-crust pie filled with smooth, slippery young coconut meat—into a tart with a nippy cheddar pastry.

METHOD

1 Make the tart dough. Sift plain flour, cake flour and salt into a bowl and whisk well to mix. Add butter and rub in with your fingertips until mixture resembles fine crumbs. Grate cheese as finely as possible into the bowl and toss well to mix it in. Sprinkle water over and stir with a spatula until dough comes together. Knead briefly to help it cohere into a ball, then wrap in plastic wrap, flatten into a disc and chill for at least 2 hours.

2 Sandwich the dough between two sheets of baking paper. Roll it out to 3 mm thickness. Chill it again for 15 minutes. Peel off paper and transfer dough to tin. Without stretching it, gently press it across the base and at least 4.5 cm up the sides. Trim edges and prick base all over with a fork. Cover with a sheet of foil, shiny side down, pressing it flush against the dough, across the base and around the sides. Chill shell for at least 6 hours. Cut any trimmings into decorative shapes for garnish, and chill them too.

3 Preheat oven to 200°C. Place a shelf in the middle position.

4 Bake tart shell for 20 minutes. Remove foil, return shell to oven and bake for 5 to 10 minutes more, until it is well browned. Transfer pan to a rack and let shell cool completely. Place any decorative trimmings on a paper-lined baking sheet and bake for 5 to 10 minutes, until browned.

5 Make the filling. Whisk coconut water, sugar, cornstarch and water chestnut starch together for 1 full minute, until smooth. Cover and let stand for 20 minutes to let the starches hydrate.

6 Strain coconut water mixture through a fine-mesh sieve into a pot, forcing through any starchy lumps. Add coconut cream, coconut flesh and salt to pot. Set pot over medium heat and stir constantly with a heatproof spatula, scraping the pot base and sides, until the mixture simmers and thickens. Taste it. It is done when the chalky

(continued on the next page)

taste of raw starch has vanished. Scrape mixture into a bowl. Scatter butter on top—it will melt and prevent a skin forming. Let filling cool to lukewarm, then whisk it to incorporate the butter.

7 Scrape the lukewarm filling into the cooled tart shell and smooth the surface. Cover with plastic wrap and chill for at least 3 hours, until the filling has set and melded to the shell.

8 Just before serving, place cutouts decoratively on top of filling. To serve, slice with a thin-bladed sharp knife. Dip it in hot water and wipe it between cuts, for neat slices.

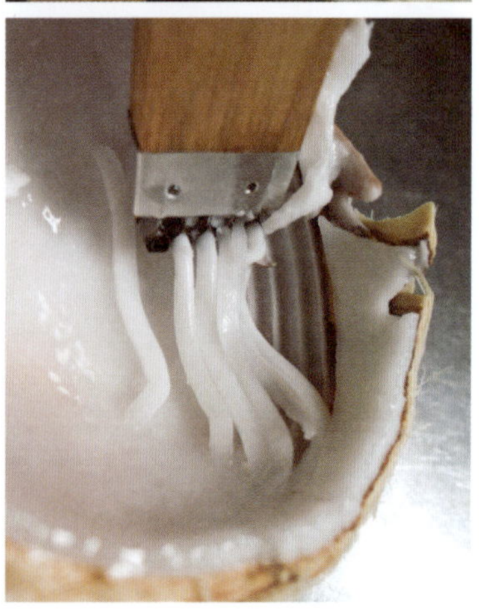

POINTERS

- Multiple rests between mixing, rolling, shaping and baking give the tart shell a crunchy, crisp texture.
- Ideally, harvest the coconut water and flesh yourself from young coconuts. You will need 1 to 2 young coconuts to obtain 1½ cups of coconut flesh. Crack them with a hammer, pestle or sturdy cleaver, then drain out the coconut water. Bash them into halves, then scrape out the flesh with a spoon—I gouge it into pasta-like strings with the handy Thai gadget pictured at lower left. Drink any leftover coconut water as cook's perk.

THAILAND

Thailand might seem an odd choice as a source of baking inspiration, as most of its traditional desserts and savouries are steamed, boiled or fried. But Thai culinary mores have been touchstones of mine for a long time: the precision of flavour balance, the attention to detail, the appreciation of how a dish strikes all five senses, the importance of context. A cardinal and continuing lesson that Thai cuisine teaches me is how sweetness and saltiness interact in both desserts and savoury preparations; how their delicate minuet is swayed or supported by pungency,

Left: *look choob, mung-bean sweets shaped like mini fruits and vegetables.*

sourness and other factors. And then there is the Thai concept of sanuk, or mindful happiness—that one should take attentive pleasure in every moment of life. What is baking if it isn't sanuk?

On a cooking and eating trip to Chiang Mai many years ago, I heard about a local cafe called Love At First Bite, and eventually tracked it down.

Footsore from traipsing side streets, my companions and I entered what looked like a private garden—eh? But yes, there it was, a small shed overflowing with ravishingly perfect camera-ready American-style desserts, everything from chocolate lava cake and pumpkin pie to individual trifles and carrot cake.

Utterly delighted, we ordered and demolished so many of them that Mattie the chef-owner came out to chat with us. An avid, self-taught baker who had lived in the US, she told us how, after resettling in Chiang Mai, her hobby became her business—a story I too know well, and which I suspect is shared by many who live to bake, bake to live, and seek sanuk.

***Left, top to bottom:** Phuket sweet potato balls as light and hollow as bubbles; young chef in training; grilled bananas. **Opposite, clockwise from top left:** watermelon at Khlong Toei market; freshly steamed sweetcorn; making roti sai mai flour crepes to wrap around candy floss; concentration is all; Love At First Bite lemon meringue pie.*

30
15
20
30

LEMON PIE
พาย มะนาว LP
บาท 45/ชิ้น 350/ถาด

BAKED SANGKHAYA FAK THONG

SERVES 6 TO 8

INGREDIENTS

1	small pumpkin, about 15 to 16 cm across
180 g	medium-thick coconut milk
100 g	Thai palm sugar
¼ tsp	salt
2	eggs
2	egg yolks

EQUIPMENT

- cake pans

POINTERS

- Kabocha and kuri squash are good for this, but use whatever small pumpkin is flavourful and in season. For best results, its flesh should be no thicker than 2 cm all around, and should not be too watery or loose-textured.
- Using a pumpkin that is squat in shape, and halving it vertically instead of horizontally, yields narrow and deep cavities for the custard, which then cooks through at the same time as the pumpkin flesh. In the wide, shallow cavities of a horizontally halved pumpkin, the custard might be overcooked by the time the pumpkin is done.
- Thai palm sugar is lighter in colour and flavour than Indonesian or Malaysian palm sugar, with a honey-like timbre. If you can only get the dark kind, mix one part of it with two parts white sugar, by weight.
- If you're lucky enough to have fresh duck eggs, use 2 duck eggs in place of the 2 chicken eggs + yolks. The custard will be extra lovely.

Sangkhaya fak thong, hollowed-out whole pumpkins filled with coconut custard then steamed, are common sights at Thai markets. I have seen variations with sliced pumpkin and custard simply mixed in a tray and steamed, then cut into squares. Either way, though it may taste good, the custard is often overcooked, with bubbles and grainy zones. I halve the pumpkin and bake it in a steamy oven instead, yielding a smoother custard with the bonus of a slightly caramelised top. The combination of rich egginess cradled in soft squash is deliriously lush.

METHOD

1 Preheat oven to 160°C. Set a shelf in the middle position. Set another shelf in the lowest position, and place on it a small cake pan half-filled with boiling water, to generate humidity.

2 Halve pumpkin vertically—i.e. cleave it through its stem end and south pole. Scrape out seeds and fibres with a sharp-edged spoon, leaving walls about 2 cm thick. Place pumpkin halves in a roasting tin or shallow cake pan. If necessary, brace their undersides with crumpled foil so that they sit firmly, without rocking.

3 Combine coconut milk, palm sugar and salt in a non-stick saucepan. Stir over medium heat until very hot and sugar has dissolved. Taste it—it should be just a tad too sweet.

STEP 2

4 Whisk eggs and egg yolks to blend in a mixing bowl. Pour in hot coconut milk mixture gradually, whisking constantly just until smooth. Strain mixture into pumpkin halves, filling them to the brim.

5 Bake pumpkin halves on the middle shelf for 45 to 55 minutes or until custards are just set—their surfaces should be lightly browned, and a toothpick inserted into their centres should emerge damp but clean. Carefully remove pan from the oven and let pumpkins cool undisturbed.

6 Serve the pumpkin warm or lightly chilled, cut into wedges, with spoons so that diners can scoop out custard and flesh together. Best eaten within 2 days of baking.

SERVES 10 TO 15

INGREDIENTS

Spice paste

5 stalks	lemongrass
3	coriander roots
1½ tbsp	finely minced peeled galangal
1½ tbsp	finely chopped garlic
1½ tbsp	finely minced shallots
1½ tbsp	hot chilli powder
1½ tsp	curry powder
3½ tbsp	fish sauce
2 tsp	palm sugar or brown sugar
1½ tsp	freshly squeezed lime or lemon juice
¾ tsp	black or white pepper
½ tsp	salt
12	kaffir lime leaves, washed
700 g	coarsely minced pork, preferably a bit fatty
40 g	panko breadcrumbs, or any dry breadcrumbs
1 tbsp	potato starch

Pastry

400 g	plain flour
½ tsp	ground tumeric
145 g	water
1 tsp	salted sugar
70 g	butter, cubed
65 g	lard or cold-pressed coconut oil (see pointers)
2	eggs
1 tsp	salt
	plain flour, for rolling
1	egg, beaten, to glaze

EQUIPMENT

- a pestle and mortar
- a stand mixer fitted with the paddle attachment
- a heavy baking sheet lined with baking paper

CHIANG MAI SAUSAGE ROLL

Smoky coils of Northern Thai sai oua sausage, served hot off the grill with herbs and greens and a mound of sticky rice, are irresistible to me. A well-integrated spice paste works serious flavour magic on fatty pork, and, over the border in Laos, on buffalo sai oua as well. Here I've wrapped a sai oua mixture in English pork-pie pastry for a giant spiralled roll that is great for toting to picnics and potlucks.

METHOD

1 Make the spice paste. Cut off and discard all but the thickest 7 cm of each lemongrass stalk. Finely slice the lemongrass across, then mince it finely; you should get about 3 tablespoons. Finely mince the coriander roots likewise. With a pestle and mortar, pound the lemongrass to a paste. Add the coriander root and pound until incorporated. Add the galangal and pound until it has broken down, then the garlic and pound likewise. Finally, add the shallots and pound until everything coheres into a smooth paste. Stir in chilli powder, curry powder, fish sauce, palm sugar, lime juice, pepper and salt. Cut away the lime leaves' thick central veins, stack the leaf blades and slice them into very fine slivers, then stir them into the spice paste.

(continued on the next page)

2 With your hands, combine spice paste, pork, breadcrumbs and potato starch in a bowl and work everything together without compacting it too much. Cover mixture tightly and chill for at least 6 hours, or overnight.

3 Make the pastry. Sift flour and turmeric into a mixing bowl and set aside. Combine water, sugar, butter and lard in a small pot, cover and set over medium heat. When it comes up to a boil, immediately take it off the heat and pour it into the flour mixture while beating constantly on low speed. Stop beating when the dough forms large clumps. Let the dough stand for 15 minutes to cool a bit, so the eggs won't cook in the next step.

4 Beat eggs and salt until well blended, then add the eggs to the dough and mix in on low speed, just until dough is smooth and homogenous. Wrap dough in plastic wrap and chill for at least 2 hours, until it firms up and relaxes.

5 Preheat oven to 180°C. Place a shelf in the middle position.

6 Divide the dough in half. Line a work surface with a sheet of baking paper. Dust one dough portion well with flour, and roll it out into a rectangle about 13 cm wide by 45 cm long, and 2 to 3 mm thick.

7 Shape half the filling into a log running lengthwise down the middle of the dough. Brush one long margin with egg, then, using the paper to assist you, flip the opposite long edge over the filling. Press the edges together tightly to seal, and trim off any excess pastry. Repeat with remaining dough and filling, to make 2 long sausage rolls in total.

8 Place one log, seam down, on the paper-lined baking sheet. Pinch one end to seal it off—this is the spiral's centre. Curl the rest of the log round it. Leave a 5 mm space between the spiral's sides—it will close up during baking. Place the second log where the first one ends, pinch all around to seal their open ends together, then continue the spiral. Lastly, pinch the outside end of the spiral to seal. Brush sausage roll all over with beaten egg.

9 Bake for 45 to 50 minutes, until the pastry is well browned and crisp.

10 Serve warm, cut into short sections or slices. If you like, partner them with Thai garnishes such as crisp white cabbage leaves, thin slices of peeled raw ginger, hot chillies and fresh herb leaves like sweet Thai basil or coriander. Leftovers are better reheated than scarfed cold out of the fridge.

POINTERS

- Grinding the spice paste in a food processor or blender will be quicker than pounding it, but I can't promise you the results will be as fragrant.
- Thai curry powder—such as Waugh's brand, which hails from England but is popular in Thailand—has keynotes of coriander, cumin, turmeric and sometimes fenugreek. Use any mild curry powder instead, or omit it if you prefer.
- Coriander roots, a foundational Thai ingredient, are snapped off whole bunches of fresh coriander. If you can't get roots, use chopped coriander stems instead.
- Neither breadcrumbs nor potato starch are authentic to sai oua, but they help to absorb some of the pork juices. Some juice and fat will inevitably seep out during the baking, but that's fine—in fact they will help the base of the roll to crisp up.
- Lard gives the pastry a tender-crisp texture and more neutral flavour; coconut oil makes it slightly crispier and lends it a coconut fragrance.

ayran

TURKEY

Turkey came at me in layers—of history and modernity, limestone and porcelain. Of revival and remaking, poetry and subtext. Of food: for instance, layers of buffalo-milk kaymak, the world's most sinful, blissful clotted cream, coiled in thick rolls like winter lawns waiting to be laid.

Or, in the window of a famous cafe, a Jenga-like tower of pastries perpetually running with caramel rivulets, refreshed by waiters constantly scooping up the puddled copper and pouring it back over the top of the stack.

Tourism campaigns frame Turkey as the nexus of East and West, but it also strives to bridge its ancient past and modern urbanity. Navigating its densely packed strata was exhausting, until I finally caught on that the best strategy was not to delve into the guidebook every two minutes. Trying to hold in mind the centuries beneath every square metre of hallowed cultural ground just gave me dizzying history-lag. Better, I decided, to dive only as deep as each moment demanded, staying nearer the surface of things.

And boy, what surfaces. Everywhere in Istanbul were dazzling patterns to catch and hold the eye. Graceful, glittering mosaics in Aya Sofya. At the famed Hacı Bekir,

founded by the creator of lokum (Turkish delight) in the 1700s, counters bedecked with arrays of the spiced, benutted and cream-stuffed confection. I spent hours wall-gazing at the Kariye Museum and the Rüstem Pasha mosque, on whose tiles shapes and colours gambolled with both decorum and zest. And oh, what things. Little familiarities leapt out from what I saw and tasted, points of resonance with things I knew from many leagues away.

In a börek's rumples and rucks were echoes of murtabak, the Indian-Muslim stuffed flatbread with which it might well share an Arabic ancestor. Gossamer-fine threads of pişmaniye cotton candy were woven with the same ancient sugar sorcery as Chinese dragon's beard and Indian sohan papdi.

At Hacı Salih, one of Istanbul's renowned traditional restaurants, I was rid forever of my (English) white sauce phobia by hünkar beğendi: bechamel sauce, roasted eggplant puree and cheese blended into a warm, swooningly scrumptious duvet for the palate. And then there was Vefa Bozacısı, a beautifully kept shop that since 1876 has brewed boza, its namesake summer drink—a tart-sweet fermented millet porridge. Served with toasted chickpeas and a dusting of cinnamon, boza looks, smells and tastes unexpectedly like applesauce, the spice hauntingly evocative of American pie... but it also glides thickly down the throat like the creamiest unfiltered Japanese nigori sake.

I dream of one day apprenticing at an old Turkish bakery or pastry shop, where I can work hands and mind, and traverse time and space, through the power of tradition.

Left, top to bottom: *intricate tilework; boza; pistachio baklava.* ***Opposite, clockwise from top left:*** *afternoon treat; cheese börek; a mosque in Ortaköy, Istanbul; Turkish chilli flakes; trimming artichokes for sale.*

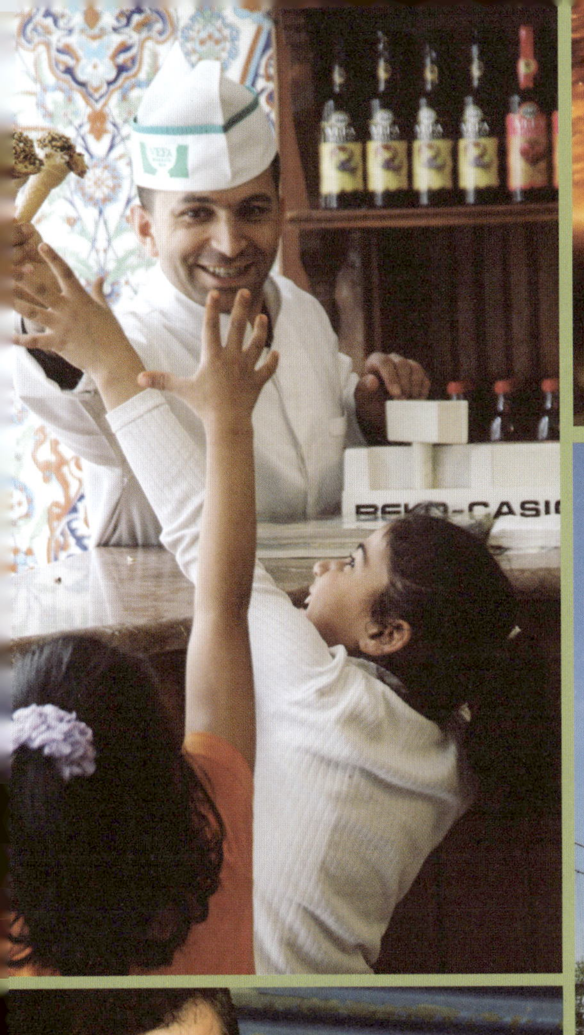

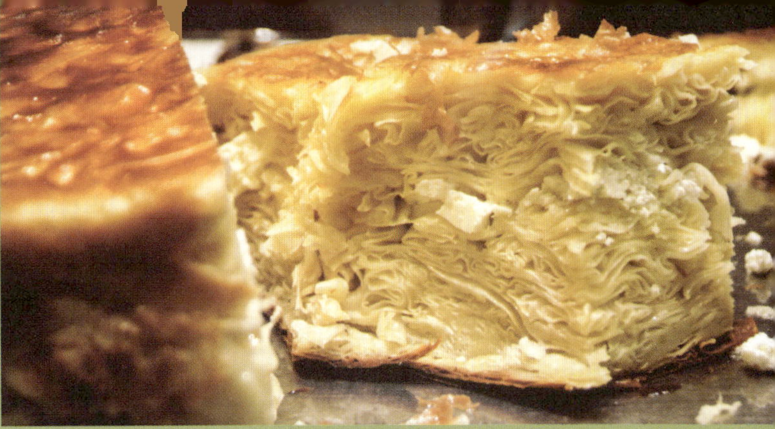

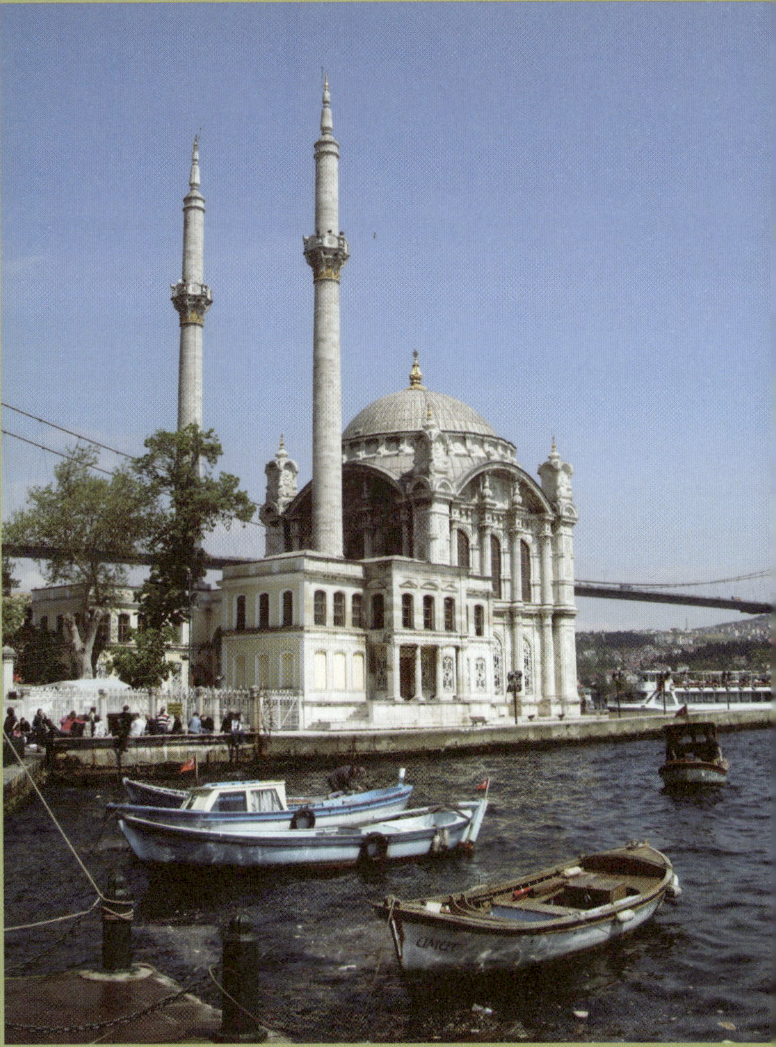

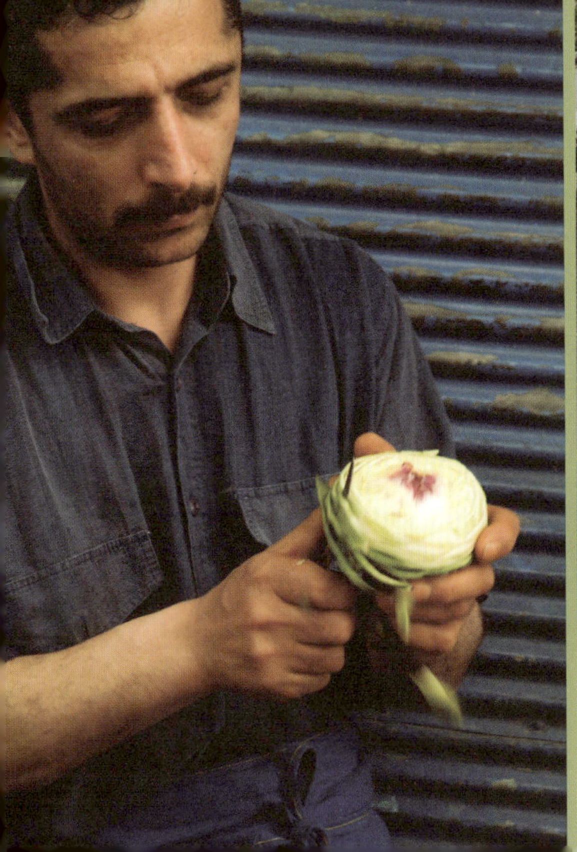

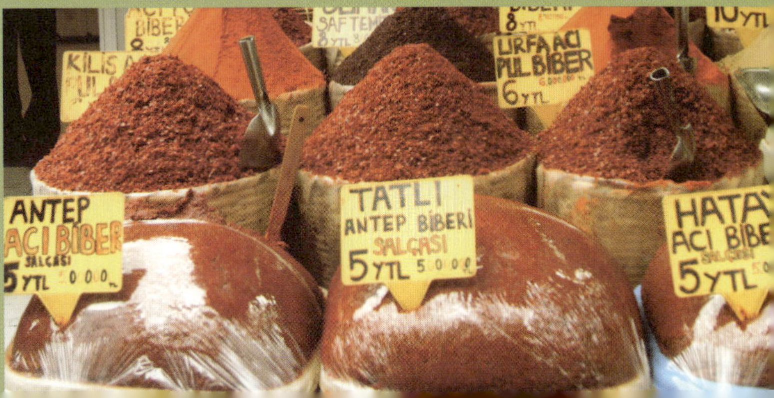
URFA ACI
PUL BIBER
6 YTL
ANTEP
ACI BIBER
SALÇASI
5 YTL
TATLI
ANTEP BİBERİ
SALÇASI
5 YTL

SERVES 2 TO 4

INGREDIENTS

5 tbsp	olive oil, plus additional for brushing
3 tbsp	tomato paste
1 tbsp	vinegar
4	garlic cloves, peeled and finely grated
2 tsp	dried thyme or oregano leaves
1 tsp	dried red chilli flakes, preferably Turkish
¾ tsp	fine sea salt
½ tsp	black pepper
½ tsp	ground cumin
500 g	king oyster or abalone mushrooms, or a mix

EQUIPMENT

- 8 to 10 wooden skewers, about 15 cm long
- a large loaf pan

MUSHROOM 'KOKOREÇ'

While rambling around the maze of uphill lanes behind Istanbul's Spice Bazaar, I passed a kebab stall grilling what appeared to be small, weirdly striated bolsters. "What is that?" I asked my friend, who replied "Kokoreç. Do you want to try some?" I did.

For a dish whose name's last syllable is pronounced 'retch', kokoreç is quite delicious. It's made by wrapping yards and yards (and yards and yards) of painstakingly cleaned lamb intestines around chunks of lamb offal on a spit, then slowly char-grilling the whole until its ruched outsides are a rich red-brown (below). To order, slices of the crusty cylinder are chopped, fried up on a griddle with herbs and tomato, and served plain or with bread (below, left). The medley of chewy, crispy, soft and friable bits, stippled with herbaceous heat, is less gamey and more winsome than you might think.

I realise that meat-free kokoreç probably isn't high on a vegan's must-have recipe list, but I didn't set out with that goal in mind. I simply wanted to find a less labour-intensive, lower-cholesterol way of mimicking kokoreç's textural pleasures at home—and mushrooms turned out to be the ticket.

METHOD

1 Combine all ingredients except mushrooms in a large bowl and whisk well to blend.

2 Wipe the mushrooms clean with a damp cloth or paper towels. Slice into pieces about 8 mm thick. Add mushrooms to mixing bowl and fold gently with a spatula to coat them with the marinade. Cover and set aside for 30 minutes at cool room temperature.

3 Soak the wooden skewers in water for 15 minutes. Preheat oven to 190°C and place a shelf in the middle position.

4 Thread the mushrooms onto skewers, cramming the pieces closely together. Place skewers across the loaf pan so that the mushrooms are suspended over its interior. Nestle skewers closely together, as the mushrooms will shrink as they cook.

5 Roast kebabs for 15 minutes. Remove pan from oven, roll skewers over to expose the underside of each kebab, and brush with olive oil. Return pan to oven and roast for 15 to 20 minutes more, until mushrooms are browned at the edges but still juicy inside. Serve hot with bread or rice, and side salads.

POINTERS

- Use flat skewers or ones with a square cross-section—mushrooms tend to slide around on round skewers.
- Thick, fleshy king oyster mushrooms and abalone mushrooms are ideal for these kebabs, as they absorb seasoning well and cook up succulent. Other contenders: chestnut or brown button mushrooms, regular oyster mushrooms, portobellos, puffballs.

POTATO-CHEESE GOZLEME

MAKES 5 GOZLEME, SERVING 5 TO 10

INGREDIENTS

Dough

350 g	plain flour, plus additional for dusting
190 g	water
70 g	plain unsweetened yoghurt
1 tbsp	olive oil, plus additional for frying
⅔ tsp	fine salt

Filling

400 g	potatoes
90 g	feta cheese, crumbled
1½ tsp	Turkish chilli flakes
2 tbsp	roughly chopped fresh mint leaves
30 g	unsalted butter, melted
	salt and black pepper

EQUIPMENT

- a heavy frying pan or griddle

Cappadocia in Central Anatolia is famous for its 'fairy chimneys', volcanic rock formations covering the landscape like postmodern patisserie. Surreal in photos, they are even stranger and more imposing up close, evoking meringues, mushrooms, sweet potatoes, half-melted sundaes. On a visit to Göreme, the region's tourist hub, my mum and I filled our eyes with the marvellous views. Unfortunately, we discovered that our bed-and-breakfast deserved a suffix of -and-get-swindled-into-a-bogus-package-tour. Deflated by a day with our sulky bogus tour guide, we walked into a random cafe with dampened moods and low expectations. Happily enough, the proprietor welcomed us like a warm ray of sunshine and restored our faith in Turkish hospitality with a big plate of gözleme.

This griddle-baked stuffed flatbread's contents vary from region to region and cook to cook, but may include vegetables, meats, cheeses and seafood. Gözleme restaurants and street stalls often feature rosy-cheeked aunties rolling out fresh dough by hand, not at all difficult to do if you go gently and slowly. Here, I've filled the chewy-soft breads with a potato-cheese mixture much like what I had in Göreme, simple but fragrant. I serve these with filfel chuma (recipe follows), which is not Turkish but is delicious made with Turkish chilli flakes.

METHOD

1 Make the dough. Sift flour into a mixing bowl. Whisk water, yoghurt, oil and salt together and pour over flour, then mix to a soft, sticky dough. Cover bowl and let dough rest for 15 minutes.

2 With lightly oiled hands, knead the rested dough gently for 5 minutes, until it is slightly more elastic, but still a bit sticky. Cover bowl and let dough rest again for 40 minutes.

3 Make the filling. Boil potatoes whole until tender. Drain, peel, and roughly crumble them into a mixing bowl. Gently fold in all remaining filling ingredients. Taste, and adjust seasoning with salt and pepper.

4 Divide the dough into 5 portions, and roll each into a ball.

5 Set your pan over medium heat. Grease it with a very thin film of oil.

6 Dust a dough ball very lightly with flour. Roll it into a round or rectangle about 40 cm across—the exact dimensions don't matter, but the dough should be extremely thin, almost thin enough to see through (far right, top).

7 Fold opposite sides of the dough to its centre, to make a long strip. Sprinkle some filling over the middle of the strip, then fold the other two sides of the dough to the centre to cover the filling, overlapping their edges slightly. Press the parcel all over to seal the open edges and even it out. Immediately lift it up and place it in the hot pan. Fry for 7 to 8 minutes, until browned on the underside, then flip it over and fry for 6 to 7 minutes more to brown the other side and finish cooking the dough through.

8 Make and fry all the gözleme likewise (far right, bottom). Serve piping hot with the filfel chuma.

FILFEL CHUMA

MAKES ABOUT 175 ML

INGREDIENTS

2 tsp	coriander seeds
1½ tsp	cumin seeds
¾ tsp	cardamom seeds (pod shells discarded)
¾ tsp	caraway seeds
70 g	garlic, peeled and finely chopped
70 g	Turkish chilli flakes (see pointers)
50 g	lukewarm water
50 g	olive oil or sunflower oil, plus additional for finishing
1 tbsp	freshly squeezed lemon juice
1 tsp	finely grated lemon zest
⅔ tsp	fine sea salt

EQUIPMENT

- a large mortar and pestle
- a spotless, airtight glass jar for storage

POINTERS

- Turkish chilli flakes, deep red and a bit oily-looking, have a complex, fruity heat which can range from mild to incendiary. Look for 'maras biber' or 'pul biber' in shops selling Turkish or Middle Eastern goods, or online. 'Urfa biber' are wine-dark flakes with mellifluous raisin, liquorice, earth and mineral notes. The nearest substitute for Turkish chilli is gochugaru, coarse chilli powder sold by Korean stores for kimchi making, although it isn't as richly nuanced.

Jerusalem, 1999. A sunny afternoon at Mahane Yehuda market. I am riveted by a spice shop's metre-long cinnamon sticks, towering cones of scarlet chilli paste, and the vigour with which Israeli auntie customers accost the young Orthodox Jewish manager. I have to get back to the tour bus parked a mad dash away, but I must buy something. I must buy something!! What, already? I grab jars of a sambal-like condiment, pay up and run. Back home in Singapore, I taste a pea-sized bead of the sambal, and my head nearly melts off my neck. I can't read the Hebrew label, but the heat haze ripples with cardamom, coriander, garlic... Years later I learn that the condiment was filfel chuma, a Libyan cousin of harissa. This is my recreation of it. Smear it on anything, carbs and bland veg especially.

METHOD

1 Roast all the spice seeds together in a dry pan over low heat for 2 to 3 minutes, shaking the pan frequently, until their aromas rise and they smell very lightly toasted. Tip them into a mortar and grind them to a fine powder with a pestle.

2 Add garlic to the mortar and pound it to a fine paste. Stir in all remaining ingredients.

3 Transfer the paste to the glass jar, and trickle a bit more oil on top. Cover and store in the fridge, where it will last for a few weeks if only touched with a clean spoon.

Left to right: *maras biber; gochugaru; urfa biber.*

4.

HYBRID VIGOUR

The theme of this section is, essentially, a key stream of the book's lifeblood: how cultural collisions can enrich your baking and cooking. Each of these recipes unites and embodies multiple traditions within the span of a few mouthfuls—I hope you will find them both hauntingly familiar and spankingly new.

BABA BABAS

Rum babas are yeasted French cake-breads tailored to be spongy and light, the better to soak up a post-bake bath of alcoholic syrup. Polish in ancestry but Parisian in their modern form, they can be very elegant if well made.

Nonetheless, I avoided them for years, not on any particular principle—rum is my go-to liquor for booze-inflected baking—but because most renditions I'd tried were sugary and flat, hardly interesting beyond the rum itself.

My mind changed when it dawned on me that a baba could be a *multi-purpose liquid conveyance vehicle*. Why just syrup and alcohol? Why not soak it in custard? In dal? In curry? Why not add a dried-fruit core to help absorb even more liquid? Behold the power of Peranakan*-Polish-French fusion!

**'Baba' is also the masculine honorific in Peranakan Malay.*

MAKES 30 BABAS

INGREDIENTS

Babas

110 g	full-cream milk, lukewarm
40 g	condensed milk
⅓ tsp	fine salt
2	egg yolks
1	egg
185 g	bread flour
10 g	potato starch
1½ tsp	instant yeast (page 15)
75 g	unsalted butter, diced and softened until just spreadable, plus additional for greasing
10	soft prunes, halved

Soaking syrup

500 g	fine sugar
150 g	light or dark muscovado sugar
700 g	water
12	cloves
12	cardamom pods
3	cinnamon sticks
½	star anise
¼	nutmeg, broken up
100 ml	dark rum, or more to taste

EQUIPMENT

- a stand or hand mixer fitted with the paddle attachment
- 30 teacake or mini-muffin pans (see pointers)
- a piping bag (no piping tip needed)

PRUNE LAPIS BABAS

Kueh lapis, aka spekkoek, is an Indonesian and Peranakan cake laden with sweet spices, butter and condensed milk, baked one painstaking layer at a time, frequently with flattened prunes embedded in them. These babas are lushly pregnant with those same flavours.

METHOD

1 Combine milk and condensed milk in a small pot, and stir over low heat until very hot but not boiling. Scrape mixture into a mixing bowl and let cool to barely lukewarm. Add salt, egg yolks and egg and whisk until smooth. Sift in bread flour and potato starch, then add yeast and mix to a sticky batter with a spatula. Cover and let stand for 15 minutes.

2 Beat batter on medium speed for 1 minute, scrape down bowl sides, and beat 1 minute more. Add butter to bowl, beat 1 minute, scrape down sides, and beat for 1 final minute. The batter should be glossy, and fall away in loose but stretchy skeins from the beater when you lift it out. Cover bowl and let proof until doubled in volume, 45 to 60 minutes.

3 Grease pans well with butter. Cut prunes into halves, or thirds if they are very large.

4 Lightly butter the inside of a piping bag. Stir down the batter and scrape it into the piping bag. Pipe batter into the pans, filling each about two-thirds full. Poke a prune piece into each pan, pushing it into its centre so that it is fully submerged in and covered by the batter. Cover the pan with greased plastic wrap and let babas proof until just doubled in size, about 15 to 20 minutes.

5 Preheat oven to 200°C. Place a shelf in the middle position.

6 Bake babas for 20 to 25 minutes, until risen and well browned. Do not underbake or they will be stodgy in the middle. Transfer pans to a rack.

7 Make syrup while babas bake. Combine all ingredients in a pot and cover, leaving lid open a crack. Bring to a simmer over medium heat, and cook for 10 to 15 minutes.

8 Transfer hot babas to a deep dish, arranging them in a single layer. Slowly ladle hot syrup over; they will gradually absorb it. Let them cool, then drizzle evenly with the rum. Cover and let stand for at least 2 hours. Serve at room temperature or lightly chilled.

POINTERS

- Metal pans yield more evenly browned babas than silicone moulds: I use individual ones, each with a 1½ tablespoon capacity. The dough will dome above them during proofing, but should not overflow.
- You can pack the babas into sterilised jars, soak them with the syrup and lots of additional rum, and keep them in the fridge for up to a couple of weeks.
- Good accompaniments: crème fraiche, clotted cream, ice cream.

GOLDEN KURMAH CUSHIONS

MAKES 18 TO 20 CUSHIONS

INGREDIENTS

100 g	hot water
40 g	evaporated milk
2 tsp	sugar
⅓ tsp	salt
2	eggs
195 g	bread flour
10 g	potato starch
1½ tsp	instant yeast (page 15)
50 g	unsalted butter, diced and softened until just spreadable, plus additional for greasing pans
	chicken kurmah (recipe follows), cooked and cooled
	chopped fresh coriander leaves, for garnish

EQUIPMENT

- a stand or hand mixer fitted with the paddle attachment
- 18 to 20 muffin pans or similar moulds
- a piping bag (no piping tip needed)

POINTERS

- The baba batter calls for evaporated milk, as you will have some left over if you've opened a can of it for the chicken kurmah. Failing this, just use 140 g warm fresh milk instead of the water + evaporated milk.
- If your moulds are individual ones, place them on a metal baking tray, spaced out.

A famous dish sold by a Singaporean catering company consists of chicken curry wrapped tightly in cellophane, then enclosed in bread dough and baked. The idea is that you broach the hot parcel, unwrap the curry and eat it with pieces of the bread. I always admired the concept, but could never quite quell disquieting thoughts of how the dough and plastic might interact, or whether the curry gets fully reheated. Solution: de-plasticise and enbaba it.

METHOD

1 Stir water, evaporated milk, sugar and salt together in a mixing bowl, and let mixture cool to lukewarm. Whisk in eggs until smooth. Sift in bread flour and potato starch, then add yeast and mix to a sticky batter with a spatula. Cover and let stand for 15 minutes.

2 Beat batter on medium speed for 1 minute, scrape down bowl sides, and beat 1 minute more. Add butter to bowl, beat 1 minute, scrape down sides, and beat for 1 final minute. The batter should be glossy, and fall away in loose but stretchy skeins from the beater when you lift it out. Cover bowl and let proof until doubled in volume, 45 to 60 minutes.

3 Grease moulds liberally with butter. Pull chicken meat off the bones, into pieces slightly smaller than your moulds—you can portion them as single chunks or agglomerated shreds.

4 Lightly butter the inside of a piping bag. Stir down the batter and scrape it into the piping bag. Pipe batter into the moulds, filling each about half full. Poke a chicken chunk into each mould, pushing it into the centre so that it is fully submerged in and covered by the batter. Cover moulds with greased plastic wrap and let babas proof until only just doubled in size, about 15 to 20 minutes.

STEP 4

5 Preheat oven to 200°C. Place a shelf in the middle position.

6 Bake babas for 22 to 24 minutes, until risen and well browned. Do not underbake them. Transfer moulds to a rack and let them cool slightly while you reheat the kurmah gravy, adding any unused chicken meat to it.

7 To serve, unmould and plate up the cushions. Let diners drench their own portions with hot kurmah gravy, and sprinkle coriander leaves on top.

SERVES 3 TO 4

INGREDIENTS

Spice paste

30 g	ginger, chopped and peeled
4 cloves	garlic, chopped
80 g	shallots, peeled and chopped
1 tbsp	ground coriander
2 tsp	ground cumin
2 tsp	ground fennel
¾ tsp	black pepper
½ tsp	ground turmeric

3 tbsp	vegetable oil
2 stalks	lemongrass, thickest 8 cm only, well bruised
1	cinnamon stick
7	cloves
8	cardamom pods
½	star anise
3	hot green chillies, slit in half lengthwise
750 g	chicken parts on the bone, skinned if desired
450 g	coconut milk
250 g	light chicken stock or water
1 tsp	salt
120 g	evaporated milk
4 tbsp	fine ground almonds
1½ tsp	freshly-squeezed lime juice, plus additional for adjusting
½ tsp	sugar, plus additional for adjusting

EQUIPMENT

- a spice grinder or pestle and mortar

CHICKEN KURMAH

Kormas are Mughal curries from North India and Pakistan, enriched with yoghurt and/or cream. Malay-style kurmahs use coconut milk instead, but have a similar flavour profile, with warmly integrated spices perfusing a rich, mellow gravy. This is one of my very favourite dishes—I could drink it by the pint.

METHOD

1 Grind all spice paste ingredients together into a fine paste with a spice grinder or pestle and mortar. If using the latter, pound the ginger smooth first, then add the garlic and pound until smooth, then the shallots similarly, and finally the dry spices.

2 Set a wok or large pan over medium heat. When hot, swirl in oil, then add spice paste, lemongrass, cinnamon, cloves, cardamom and star anise. Fry, stirring constantly, for 5 to 6 minutes, until paste has thickened and darkened, and starts to smell toasty.

3 Add green chillies and chicken parts and fry for 2 minutes, stirring to coat the chicken with the spices. Add coconut milk, stock and salt, and bring to a boil. Cover pan, reduce heat to maintain a simmer, and cook for 50 to 60 minutes, until chicken is tender.

4 Stir in evaporated milk, almonds, lime juice and sugar. Boil gently, uncovered, for 5 minutes more. Taste gravy and adjust seasoning with more salt, sugar or lime juice as needed; it should be rich but not overly cloying. Let cool before using for the cushions.

POINTERS

- You can make the kurmah the day before you bake the babas, keeping it chilled until needed. I suggest separating the chicken and gravy before chilling, as the latter will solidify when cold. You don't want to root around messily in the jellied gravy for the meat.

This serving plate is actually a spoon rest. Used to cradle a sauce-soaked cushion, it lets me channel every last precious drop of gravy into my waiting mouth.

THE WORLD OF SUSI PANG

Lightly spiced minced pork snuggled in velvety sweet potato dough, pang susi are little buns from the Eurasian communities in Singapore and Melaka, Malaysia, whose heritage and cuisine are a historical salmagundi of Portuguese, Dutch, Indian, Malay and Chinese influences. They were familiar to my parents' and grandparents' generations, and were, if not widespread, at least predictably found at Singapore's old-school bakeries up until the early 1990s. Now quite endangered, confined mostly to private homes and heritage cookbooks, they are far too good not to be revived.

They are also rather mysterious, as I discovered while trying to trace their backstory.

'Pang' derives from the Iberian 'pan', meaning bread, but no Eurasian I spoke to could tell me the meaning of 'susi', or anything else about the buns bar their iconic status.

Advice from a Portuguese history scholar and elusive library texts led me to tantalising facts, but few concrete connections:

- In the autonomous Portuguese Azores Islands, traditional sweet-potato scones called broinhas de Natal are made at Christmas. Though containing neither meat nor yeast, they seem to be the only extant Portuguese baked goods that look exactly like pang susi, which are also eaten at Christmas.
- From the 1500s onwards, along with many from the mainland, Azoreans were among the scores of Portuguese who emigrated to the Asian colonies, including Macau and Melaka.
- Classic pang susi filling is almost identical to minchi, an emblematic Macanese Eurasian dish.
- To make paezinhos recheados, 'stuffed buns', Macanese cooks hollow out small baked wheat-flour buns, fill them with minchi, then deep-fry or re-bake them until hot.
- Could 'paezinho' have elided into 'pang susi' over the course of centuries? It doesn't seem all that plausible, even if you squint your eardrums.

Too many jigsaw pieces in search of a puzzle frame... But how blessed we are to have the final picture to enjoy.

Both pages, clockwise from top left:
a church on Coloane Island, Macau; traditonal pang susi; Portuguese restaurants on Taipa Island, Macau; church breakfast.

"SI FUNG" CHURRASCO
豐燒烤
RUA DOS CLERIGOS
CAFE GALO
啡美食

PANG SUSI

Traditional hand-kneaded pang susi dough is sweet, rich and a little heavy from the spuds and butter. I have used fairly classic ingredient ratios, but tweaked the mixing method for a lighter-textured bun, so that you can eat more pang susi without feeling like a loaded aircraft carrier. I've given two alternative filling options, one old and one new.

MAKES 22 TO 24 PANG SUSI

INGREDIENTS

Dough

1	large orange-fleshed sweet potato (about 300 g)
90 g	unsalted butter, cubed
40 g	caster sugar
2 tbsp	milk
1 tsp	salt
2	egg yolks
2 tsp	brandy
300 g	bread flour, plus additional for dusting
2 tsp	osmotolerant or regular instant yeast (page 15)
	one batch pang susi filling (recipes follow), cooked and cooled

Glaze

1	egg white
2 tsp	milk
½ tsp	cornstarch
¼ tsp	sugar

EQUIPMENT

- a stand mixer fitted with the dough hook, or elbow grease
- baking sheets lined with baking paper

POINTERS

- The dough for the curry debal buns on page 205 was made with purple-fleshed sweet potatoes instead of orange ones. They are less moist, so you may need to increase the milk or water quantity a bit to compensate.
- The curry debal buns were also baked in round muffin tins—this may lengthen the baking time by a couple of minutes.

METHOD

1 Steam the sweet potato until very tender, then peel and mash finely. Weigh out 200 g of mash into a mixing bowl, and while it is still piping hot, add the butter, sugar, milk and salt, and beat hard with a whisk until smooth. Let mixture cool to room temperature, then beat in egg yolks and brandy.

2 Add bread flour and yeast to the sweet potato mixture. Stir with a spatula to make a plasticine-like dough. Cover bowl with a damp tea towel and let it stand at room temperature for 20 minutes.

3 Knead the dough for 1 minute on medium-low speed. (If kneading by hand, use the stretch-fold technique—see page 30). Re-cover bowl and let dough rest for 5 minutes. Knead for another 1 to 2 minutes, until dough is elastic. It will still be sticky and will not entirely clean the bowl sides. Scrape dough into a clean bowl lightly greased with oil, cover it, and let rise at room temperature until doubled in size, 1 to 2 hours.

4 Turn dough out onto a lightly oiled work surface. Gently deflate it by pressing it all over. Divide it into 30 g pieces—you should get 22 to 24 of them. Roll each piece into a ball. Cover balls with plastic wrap and let them relax for 10 minutes.

5 On a lightly floured work surface, roll a dough ball into a disc about 9 cm wide. Top with a tablespoonful of filling, then fold dough in half and pinch seam well to seal. Shape the bun like a fat rugby ball, pinching the seam ends to taper them, and place on baking sheets, seam side down. Make all buns likewise, spacing them at least 5 cm apart. Cover with greased plastic wrap and let rise until barely doubled, 45 to 60 minutes.

6 Preheat oven to 185°C. Place shelves in the upper and lower thirds of the oven.

7 Make the glaze by whisking all ingredients together until smooth—strain it if it is lumpy. Uncover buns and brush them gently with the glaze. Bake for 12 minutes, then quickly swap sheets between shelves to help buns bake more evenly. Bake for 4 to 7 minutes more, until risen and golden.

8 Transfer sheet to a rack and let the pang susi cool slightly. Serve warm or at room temperature. Leftovers will keep, loosely wrapped and refrigerated, for 2 to 3 days.

MAKES ENOUGH FOR 22 TO 24 PANG SUSI

INGREDIENTS

1 tbsp	oil
125 g	brown-skinned onion, peeled and diced
2 tsp	chopped garlic
1	cinnamon stick
1	small star anise
4	cloves
400 g	minced pork, at room temperature
1½ tsp	dark soy sauce
¼ tsp	ground nutmeg
	salt
¾ tsp	cornstarch, dissolved in 1 tbsp water

CLASSIC PANG SUSI FILLING

METHOD

1 Set a wok or heavy-based saucepan over medium-high heat. When hot, swirl in oil, then add onions, garlic, cinnamon, star anise and cloves. Fry for 2 to 3 minutes, stirring, until onions are softened and starting to brown.

2 Add pork to pan and fry briskly, breaking up clumps, until pork is lightly browned. Add soy sauce and nutmeg, stir well, reduce heat to medium and cover pan. Cook for 6 to 10 minutes, lifting the lid and stirring a couple of times, until the pork is tender and has released a little juice.

3 Taste and adjust seasoning with salt, then stir in cornstarch mixture and cook for a minute more, until the juices thicken and cling to the pork. Scrape filling into a bowl, cover and let cool completely.

POINTERS

- Some recipes add diced potato, but I prefer this filling without them.

CURRY DEBAL PANG SUSI FILLING

Curry debal, also known as devil curry, is another Eurasian dish, closely related to Macanese diabo, and more distantly to the fiery, vinegary curries of Goa like sorpatel and vindalho. Debal and diabo are both made with roast meats leftover from festive banquets, re-cooked together with onions, chillies and spices into a gloriously potent stew to be ladled generously over rice. This new-wave pang susi filling is my precis of the original dish, equally punchy but tailored for smaller doses.

MAKES ENOUGH FOR 22 TO 24 PANG SUSI

INGREDIENTS

Spice paste

1½ tbsp	finely minced lemongrass
1 tbsp	finely chopped galangal
3	candlenuts or cashew nuts
4	garlic cloves
1 tbsp	hot chilli powder, or to taste
1 tbsp	water

1½ tbsp	oil
5 strips	streaky bacon, finely diced
2 tsp	black mustard seeds
110 g	purple onion, thinly sliced
1 large	red chilli, finely shredded
1½ tbsp	finely shredded ginger
400 g	minced chicken
4 tbsp	water
3 tbsp	vinegar, plus additional for adjusting (see pointers)
1 tbsp	prepared English mustard
1 tsp	dark soy sauce
1 tsp	brown sugar, plus additional for adjusting
	salt
¾ tsp	cornstarch, dissolved in 1 tbsp water

EQUIPMENT

- a pestle and mortar, small blender or a spice grinder

POINTERS

- Use a mild but characterful vinegar—a good apple cider vinegar, brown rice vinegar, or cane vinegar.
- If the chicken gives off a lot of liquid as it fries, omit the water.

METHOD

1 Grind all the spice paste ingredients together into a fine paste with a spice grinder or pestle and mortar. If using the latter, pound them sequentially in the order given, pounding each spice smooth before adding the next.

2 Set a wok or heavy-based pan over medium-high heat. When hot, swirl in oil, then add bacon. Stir-fry until lightly browned, then scoop out bacon onto a plate, leaving the fat in the wok.

3 Add spice paste and mustard seeds to wok. Fry for 2 to 3 minutes, stirring constantly, until paste thickens slightly and starts to smell caramelised. Add onion, chilli and ginger and fry briskly for 1 minute. Add chicken and fry for 2 minutes more, breaking up clumps, until chicken is opaque. Stir in bacon, water, vinegar, mustard, soy sauce and sugar, reduce heat to medium, cover and cook for 10 minutes.

4 Uncover the wok, taste and adjust seasoning with salt, and more sugar or vinegar if needed. Stir in cornstarch slurry and cook for a minute more, until the simmering juices thicken and cling to the chicken. Scrape filling into a bowl and let cool completely.

THE CROWN IN THE JEWEL

One of the best things about multi-ethnic Singapore is its crowded public holiday calendar. Someone's always celebrating something, and celebrations mean *food*.

My earliest memories of Indian grub go far back: exchanging goodies with Sikh neighbours at Deepavali (Diwali) and Chinese New Year; indelicately plunging my chubby fingers into biryani rice at a banana-leaf wedding meal. Indian films were another gateway drug to Indian food, thanks to the kachang puteh—nut and lentil snacks in paper cones—mandatorily munched by filmgoers. Crunch and spice and catchy music and vivid Technicolor combined to totally transfix me.

Left: *Making a coconut-stuffed modak, a steamed Indian dumpling.*

Later, living in Britain, I was gripped by the splendours of Northern Indian dishes and the irreverence of Anglo-influenced Indian food. The long historical entanglement of India and the UK has had consequences both grievous and good, but the edible ones surely belong to the latter category.

During the days of Empire, Anglo-Indian cuisine arose as a collusion between British and European immigrants' tastebuds, and the skills of the khansamas, Indian cooks, whom they employed. Thus were born dishes like country captain curry, mulligatawny soup and kedgeree.

When the British Raj ended and the sahibs returned home, the cross-pollination continued, yielding such treasures as Worcestershire sauce (go look it up). When later tides of immigration reversed direction, bringing Indian culture and food to the UK, things got even more diverse, with English Indian restaurant food becoming a subgenre of its own, for better (chicken tikka masala) or for worse (face-dissolving phaal curries).

I have indelible memories of Birmingham's baltis and torso-sized naans, sterling onion bhajis from an ultra-modern Punjabi deli, stupendous lamb samosas with a sharp mint sauce at a Commonwealth Fair in London, and three kinds of fresh pilau at my local Sainsbury's. (Haggis pakoras I have not yet tried, but they are on my bucket list.) The following recipes are my tribute to this most fertile and spicy of seedbeds.

Left, top to bottom: *petting a cow at spring festival; expert chapati makers; sundries at dusk.* ***Opposite, clockwise from top left:*** *bargaining for bananas; Birmingham balti-house naan; film stars are watching you; syrup-soaked jalebis.*

GOBI CHEESE MANCHURIAN

My torrid love for gobi manchurian goes beyond all rationality. The combination of deep-fried cauliflower, tossed with green chillies, garlic, onion and a soy-vinegar sauce, is a 'Chindian' fusion dish invented in the 1970s by a Chinese restaurateur in Mumbai. Undeniably tasty, but all too often the kind of greasy-corner-takeaway dish in which glaringly high-key, palate-blitzing flavours trump actual quality. My mind knows this, and looks on askance. My heart dives in unreservedly, like a young child into the IKEA plastic ball pit. In this arranged marriage of an English-style cauliflower cheese and a manchurian sauce, the former's mellow richness plays Mills to the latter's energetic Boon.

SERVES 4 TO 6

INGREDIENTS

1 head	cauliflower (about 800g)

Cheese sauce

400 g	milk
50 g	whipping cream
30 g	roasted cashew nuts, pounded to a paste, or cashew nut butter
2 tsp	potato starch
½ tsp	lemon juice
175 g	cheddar cheese, grated
	salt and pepper

Manchurian sauce

3 tbsp	chilli sauce (see pointers)
2 tbsp	water
1½ tbsp	light soy sauce
2 tsp	tomato ketchup
1½ tsp	Chinkiang black vinegar (see pointers)
½ tsp	cornstarch
1 tbsp	oil, plus additional for greasing
1	hot green chilli, finely chopped
2 tbsp	minced peeled shallots
2 tsp	minced garlic
1½ tsp	minced ginger

EQUIPMENT

- a baking tray
- a shallow ovenproof dish or casserole

STEP 2

METHOD

1 Measure out and prep all your ingredients before you do anything else. Preheat oven to 190°C. Place a shelf in the upper third of the oven. Lightly grease baking tray with oil.

2 Cut the cauliflower into 2 cm-thick slices, or break it into medium-sized florets. Place on oiled tray, and bake for 15 to 20 minutes, until just tender and starting to brown in places. Do not over-cook it or it will be limp and soulless.

3 While the cauliflower bakes, make the cheese sauce. Combine milk, cream, cashew nut paste, and potato starch in a saucepan, and whisk until smooth. Set pan over medium heat and bring to a simmer, whisking constantly. Simmer for about 1 minute, until sauce thickens to a custard-like consistency. Take the pan off the heat. Whisk in the lemon juice, then add 140 g of the grated cheese, a couple of tablespoons at a time, whisking until smooth before adding the next portion. Season to taste with salt and pepper, being mindful that the sauce will contrast with punchy manchurian gravy.

4 Transfer the cauliflower to the ovenproof dish, snuggling pieces closely. Pour over the cheese sauce, shaking the dish to settle it into the nooks and crannies. Sprinkle over the remaining 35 g of grated cheese. Place dish in the oven and bake for 10 minutes, until the cheese has melted and browned in spots.

5 Make manchurian sauce while the gobi cheese bakes. Whisk chilli sauce, water, soy sauce, ketchup, vinegar and cornstarch together in a bowl until smooth, and set aside. Heat oil in a small pot over medium heat. When hot, add chilli, shallots, garlic and ginger and stir-fry for about 2 minutes, just until shallots have softened and are beginning to brown. Add sauce mixture to pan and simmer for several seconds more, until thickened.

6 Spoon manchurian sauce over the browned gobi cheese. Serve piping hot, yaar.

POINTERS

- Use a sweetish chilli sauce that is not too tart, so it will properly balance the vinegar and soy sauce.
- Chinese Chinkiang black vinegar gives the sauce particular depth. If you can't get it, substitute (cheap) balsamic, brown rice, or regular rice vinegar.
- Bechamel-based cheese sauce is easily ruined by a botched roux. Thickened with cashew nuts instead, my easier but equally suave cheese sauce is inspired by a gobi recipe in *Cook Indian* by Mrs P Majumder, a classic Singapore heritage cookbook.

MAKES 4 PASTIES

INGREDIENTS

Pastry

250 g	plain flour, plus additional for dusting
250 g	bread flour
¾ tsp	salt
120 g	cold unsalted butter, cut into small pieces
65g	firm, cold fat (see pointers), cut into small pieces
150 g	cold water

Filling

100 g	chorizo, cut into thin half-moons
1	brown-skinned onion, chopped
2 tsp	finely chopped garlic
1½ tsp	finely chopped ginger
275 g	pork collar
200 g	peeled potatoes
1 tbsp	water
2 tsp	vinegar (see pointers)
1½ tsp	hot chilli powder
1 tsp	smoked paprika
½ tsp	black pepper
½ tsp	ground cumin
½ tsp	ground cinnamon
¼ tsp	ground turmeric
⅛ tsp	ground cloves or ground nutmeg
½ tsp	salt
	beaten egg, for glazing

EQUIPMENT

- a stand mixer fitted with the paddle attachment, or two hands
- a baking sheet lined with baking paper

GOANISH PASTIES

A Goan chef came to our house for dinner one time. Serious-minded and intense, Antoinette brought with her lively stories and strong opinions—"Why do these young chefs play with spices before they know them properly? It took me two years to understand cumin alone!" Best of all, she also brought a bag of homemade sausages sent over by an aunt in Goa. We simmered the brick-red links with thickly sliced potatoes and onions in a big pot of water, and once everything was cooked through, lifted them out and devoured them all together. Seldom have I fallen so hard and so fast for anything as I did for those sausages, bursting with vermilion fat, their deep-seated meatiness shot through with pepper, clove and the bright sting of vinegar. I've not had their like since. In their stead, I've combined the same flavours with another of my all-time loves—a Cornish pasty.

METHOD

1 Make the pastry. Sift flours into a mixing bowl, add salt and whisk well to mix. Add butter and fat pieces. Rub the fat into the flour with the mixer paddle on low speed, or with your fingers, until it disperses and the mixture looks like fine crumbs. Pour in the cold water and mix on low speed, or stir with a spatula, until a slightly elastic dough forms. Turn it out and knead it briefly by hand, just until you feel the moisture is evenly distributed. Shape dough into a thick disc, wrap in plastic wrap and chill for at least 4 hours or overnight.

2 Make the filling. Fry chorizo in a pan over medium heat until some of its fat renders, 1 to 2 minutes. Add onion, garlic and ginger and fry for 1 minute more, just until the onion starts to soften. Transfer mixture to a bowl and let it cool.

3 Cut pork into 1 cm dice. Cut potatoes into thumbnail-sized squares, about 4 mm thick. Combine pork, potato and chorizo mixture with all remaining filling ingredients and mix well.

4 Preheat oven to 200°C. Place a shelf in the middle position.

5 Lightly flour a work surface. Cut dough disc into quarters. Roll one portion into a 25 cm circle, rotating dough between strokes so that it flattens evenly, with no thinner or thicker spots.

(continued on the next page)

POINTERS

- Goan vinegar is made from toddy (see page 53). The best substitute is palm or coconut vinegar from the Philippines or elsewhere, or a good cider, cane or rice vinegar.
- Lard is my preferred fat, but you can also use rendered beef fat, or coconut oil that has been measured out and then frozen until firm. Failing any of these, just use more butter.
- Bread flour gives the pastry strength, so it can cradle the moist filling without cracking or bursting, and bake up crisp and domed.
- These pasties bake most evenly in fan-assisted ovens.

6 Place a quarter of the filling in a semi-circular mound on the upper half of the circle, leaving a finger-wide margin. Dampen the margin, then fold the dough over to enclose the filling, cupping your hands around it to expel any air, as you press the margin to seal. Trim the edge with a sharp knife, to leave a neat, semi-circular rim about 2 cm wide.

7 Starting at one corner of the rim, fold over successively overlapping short sections, using your thumbs. Whether you crimp clockwise or anticlockwise round the curve, the leading front thumb folds, and the following thumb presses to seal. Resist the urge to stretch the pastry as you crimp—this could create weak points that then leak.

8 Make all pasties likewise. Place them on the baking sheet and brush them with beaten egg. Bake for 20 minutes, then lower heat to 165°C and bake for another 30 to 35 minutes, until golden. Serve hot.

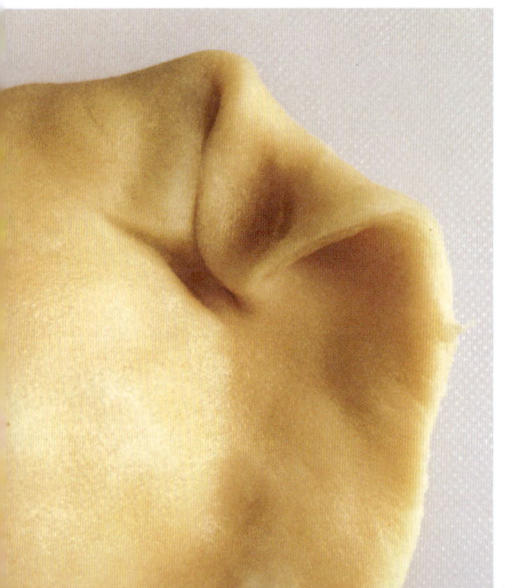

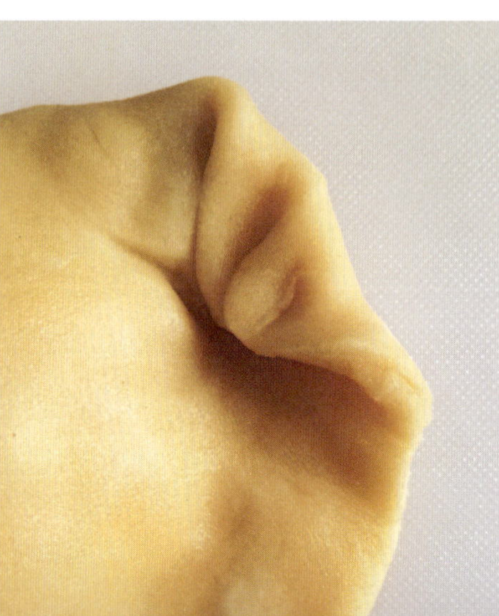

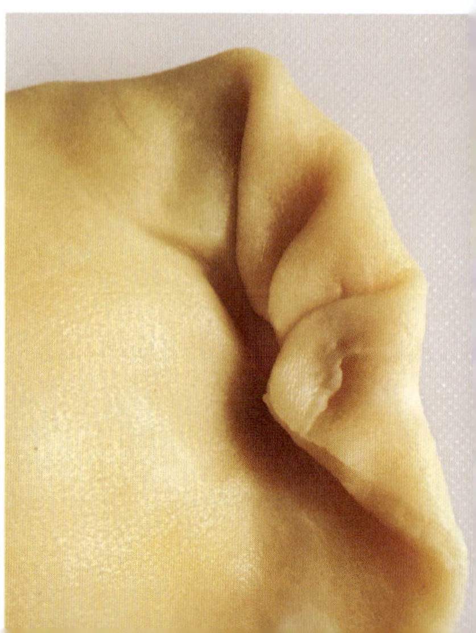

SERVES 4 TO 6

INGREDIENTS

95 g	freshly squeezed lime juice
100 g	sugar
tiny pinch	salt
300 g	whipping cream
1 tbsp	finely grated lime zest, plus additional for garnish
	fancy salt, for garnish

EQUIPMENT

- 4 to 6 glasses or ramekins, each about 150 ml capacity
- an instant-read thermometer

POINTERS

- Don't even think of ready-squeezed juice—the zing of the freshly squeezed is crucial to this recipe. Pictured on the right are different limes I've found at Indian groceries—most classic to nimbu pani are the small round yellow ones, known as key limes elsewhere in the world, floral and sour. Any lime can be used instead, so long as it has no bitter aftertaste.

NIMBU PANI POSSET

Possets are very old and traditional English desserts made of sweetened cream, curdled into light but luscious gels with the help of an alcohol and/or acid. I've long wondered why they aren't as popular as the far more fiddly panna cotta. For this posset, I've used nimbu pani, Indian limeade, as the setting agent—its little hit of salt is the perfect counterpoint.

METHOD

1 Combine lime juice, sugar and salt in a pot. Set over low heat and stir until mixture comes to a simmer and sugar dissolves completely. Cover and keep warm.

2 Combine cream and zest in a small, heavy-based pot. Place over medium-low heat and heat, stirring occasionally, until it just comes up to the boil. Do not let it actually boil. Strain cream through a sieve into a clean bowl.

3 Pour lime syrup into the cream, whisking constantly to blend. Ladle the mixture into serving glasses. Let cool to room temperature, then cover and chill for at least 4 hours or until set. To serve, garnish with a few grains of salt—I've used blueberry-infused salt in the photo overleaf—and grated lime zest, and serve with the Shrewsbury biscuits.

MAKES 25 TO 35 BISCUITS

INGREDIENTS

145 g	plain flour
65 g	icing sugar
30 g	cornstarch
¾ tsp	ground cardamom
¾ tsp	ground ginger
⅔ tsp	white pepper
2 tsp	finely grated lime or lemon zest
⅓ tsp	fine salt
125 g	cold unsalted butter, cut into small cubes
1	egg yolk

EQUIPMENT

- a mixer fitted with the paddle attachment
- baking sheets lined with baking paper

SPICED SHREWSBURY BISCUITS

Shrewsbury biscuits are buttery, crisp delicacies from Shropshire, and one of the world's most famous places to get them is...Pune, Maharashtra. Souvenirs of the British era, the biscuits were adopted as signature items by the city's bakeries in the 1920s, and have been roaringly popular ever since. Today's Pune editions are slightly smaller than the English originals, but still beloved for their butteriness. To that template I have added an edited gingerbread spice blend—minus the usual cola-like top notes of cinnamon and nutmeg, the ginger, cardamom and pepper sparkle like clean cricket whites.

METHOD

1 Sift flour, icing sugar, cornstarch, cardamom, ginger and pepper into a mixing bowl. Add grated zest and salt and beat on low speed until thoroughly blended, about 1 minute.

2 Add butter to bowl and beat for 1 to 2 minutes on low speed, until it has dispersed and mixture resembles fine crumbs. Add egg yolk to bowl, and beat until dough comes together into a ball. Stop beating, and knead dough briefly with your hands to even it out. Wrap dough in plastic wrap and chill for at least 6 hours or overnight.

3 Preheat oven to 180°C. Place a shelf in the middle position.

4 Roll the dough out 4 mm thick, and cut out small biscuits in whatever shape you desire. Alternatively, roll the dough into small balls, and flatten them—I shaped the biscuits shown here by stamping 20 g balls of dough into 4 mm-thick discs, which I then cut in half to resemble citrus wedges. Place biscuits on baking sheets, spacing them 2 cm apart, and bake for 11 to 13 minutes (in batches, one sheet at a time, if necessary), until pale golden and cooked through. Do not underbake.

5 Transfer baking sheets to cooling racks. As soon as biscuits are completely cool, transfer them to an airtight container.

SERVES 4

INGREDIENTS

200 g	water
2	cassia or cinnamon sticks, broken into small fragments
12	cardamom pods
10	cloves
½ tsp	black peppercorns
¼	nutmeg, in fragments
2½ tbsp	black tea leaves
80 g	condensed milk
250 g	milk (see pointers)
80 g	old ginger

EQUIPMENT

- 4 glasses or ramekins, each about 150 ml capacity
- an instant-read thermometer

POINTERS

- The ginger must be freshly grated and juiced—its posset-setting power wanes if it waits around. Use thick-skinned, plump-bodied old ginger.
- High-calcium, low-fat milk yields a slightly firmer posset; full-cream milk gives a more tenuous but more velvety texture, as fat weakens the gel slightly.
- To serve the possets cold, let them cool completely, cover them with plastic wrap, and chill for an hour or so. Serve them within 24 hours.

MASALA CHAI POSSET

Strictly speaking, this is an Anglo-Sino-Indian dessert. I've added masala chai's warmth to an iconic Hong Kong dessert—ginger milk pudding (hot sweetened milk mixed with freshly-squeezed ginger juice). The ginger's protease enzymes act on milk proteins to form a posset so fragile, so ethereal, that it's more like the idea of custard than actual custard—it should shiver apart into tiny, silken curds even as you dunk in the oat snaps.

METHOD

1 Combine water and all the spices in a small pot with a tight-fitting lid. Cover and bring to a simmer over low heat. Simmer for 5 minutes, then add the tea leaves, cover, and simmer very gently for 4 to 5 minutes. The infusion should be potent and aromatic.

2 Strain tea into a clean pot, pressing on the solids to extract as much liquid as possible. Add condensed milk and milk, and whisk well to blend. Set aside momentarily.

3 Scrape the skin off the ginger with the edge of a spoon. Grate ginger very finely, then squeeze out its juice. Strain the juice through a fine-mesh strainer. Place 1½ teaspoons of ginger juice in each glass.

4 Set the masala chai over medium-low heat. Monitoring it with the thermometer, bring it just up to 65°C—higher temperatures will weaken the set.

5 Ladle the chai into each glass, pouring from a height so that it mingles thoroughly with the ginger juice—do not stir once it is in the glass, as this disrupts the set. Let the possets stand undisturbed for 15 minutes, until lightly gelled. Serve immediately, while warm.

CORIANDER OAT SNAPS

Coriander's scorched-orange nuances suit the thin-and-crisp snap biscuit format beautifully. If possible, use lightly toasted, freshly ground coriander seeds to maximise their citrus aspect, which the orange extract further underlines.

MAKES ABOUT 40 SNAPS

INGREDIENTS

90 g	unsalted butter
2 tbsp	golden syrup or maple syrup
½ tsp	salt
1 tbsp	ground coriander
55 g	sugar
1	egg white
⅛ tsp	orange extract (optional)
60 g	plain flour
½ tsp	baking powder
100 g	oatmeal (see pointers)

EQUIPMENT

- baking sheets lined with baking paper

POINTERS

- I like a medium-coarse stone-ground oatmeal—sometimes labelled 'Scottish'—for these. Alternatively, grind rolled oats to a similar consistency in a blender. Avoid steel-cut or instant oats, respectively too chunky and too insubstantial.

METHOD

1 Stir butter, golden syrup and salt together in a small pot over low heat, until butter has just melted. Add coriander and stir well, then take pot off heat. Stir in sugar. Let mixture cool until tepid, then stir in egg white and orange extract.

2 Sift flour and baking powder into a mixing bowl, then add oatmeal and whisk well to blend. Scrape butter mixture into bowl and stir with a spatula to make a soft, sticky dough. Cover bowl with plastic wrap and chill dough for at least 4 hours.

3 Preheat oven to 165°C. Place a shelf in the middle position.

4 Spoon teaspoons of dough onto a baking sheet. With the back of a wet spoon, or damp fingertips, smear the dough out into oblongs about 7 cm long and 2 to 3 mm thick, leaving at least 1cm space between them. Bake snaps in multiple batches, one sheet at a time, for about 12 minutes per batch, until deep golden brown.

5 Transfer baking sheets to racks to cool. As soon as the snaps are completely cool and crisp, transfer them to an airtight container.

SAMOANAKAN

Pani popo are Samoan buns. Made of a plain dough, they are proofed while snuggled closely in a pan, drenched with a thickened and sweetened coconut milk sauce, then sent into the oven. As they bake, the sauce keeps their skins moist and the ambient atmosphere humid, helping the buns expand into fluffy orbs. By the time they are done, the sauce has formed a wafer-thin brown crust on their upper surfaces, and pools of creamy gel underneath them.

Reading about pani popo got my heart pounding and my arteries creaking, not to mention activating my innate Peranakan instinct for taking a rich dish even further over the top. All that these beauties needed to really go into overdrive, I reckoned, was a filling.

SAMBAL HAYBEE PANI POPO

When I was growing up, my family fridge almost always had a Tupperware of sambal haybee in it. It's the kind of side dish-cum-condiment that, if you're going to make a little of, you might as well make a lot of. It goes perfectly with a rice and curry meal, or on top of rice congee, or (my favourite) in a folded slice of buttered white bread. These pani popo are an exaltation of that childhood sandwich, made in the same triangular shape. They are superb for picnics.

MAKES 16 LARGE BUNS

INGREDIENTS

Dough

180 g	milk
20 g	potato starch
40 g	sugar
¾ tsp	salt
1	egg
40 g	unsalted butter, diced, plus additional for greasing pans
220 g	plain flour, plus additional for dusting
120 g	bread flour
1½ tsp	instant yeast (page 15)
1 cup	sambal haybee (recipe follows)

Coconut milk sauce

380 g	coconut milk
25 g	sugar
2 tsp	cornstarch
⅓ tsp	salt

EQUIPMENT

- a stand mixer fitted with the dough hook, or two hands and some stamina
- two shallow 23cm one-piece round pie pans or cake tins

POINTERS

- Use coconut milk of medium thickness, similar to the consistency of evaporated milk—not coconut cream, which is too rich, or thin coconut milk, which ain't no fun nohow.
- If you're feeling really fancy, tuck hard-boiled egg wedges into the buns along with the sambal haybee.

METHOD

1 Combine milk, potato starch, sugar, salt and egg in a small pot and whisk until smooth. Set over medium-low heat and cook, whisking constantly, until thickened into a gloopy custard. Add butter and whisk until melted and incorporated. Let mixture cool completely.

2 Whisk plain flour, bread flour and yeast together. Stir in custard to make a shaggy, stiff dough. Cover bowl with a damp tea towel. Let stand at room temperature for 25 minutes.

3 Knead the dough on medium-low speed for 1 minute. Re-cover bowl with the tea towel and let dough rest for 5 minutes. Repeat the kneading and resting twice more, by the end of which the dough should be fairly elastic (it is slightly stiffer than other doughs in this book). Re-cover bowl with the tea towel. Let dough proof until doubled in size, 60 to 90 minutes.

4 Lightly flour a work surface. Turn out dough and press gently to deflate. Dust dough with flour and roll it out into a 34 cm square. Roll slowly and smoothly, rotating the dough frequently, so that it extends without snapping back.

5 Cut the dough into 16 equal small squares. Place 1 tablespoon of sambal haybee on a square, then fold it in half diagonally to make a triangle. Pinch edges well to seal. Make all buns likewise.

6 Lightly grease pans with butter. Fan out 8 buns in each pan like a pinwheel, with short corners overlapping slightly. Let rise at room temperature until puffy and nearly doubled in size, about 30 minutes.

7 Make the sauce while buns rise. Combine all ingredients in a small pot, and cook over medium-low heat for 5 to 8 minutes, stirring constantly, until it comes to a simmer and thickens slightly. Take pot off the heat, cover it and set it aside.

8 Preheat oven to 180°C. Place shelves in the upper and lower thirds of the oven.

9 Ladle warm sauce evenly over buns. Bake for 15 minutes, swap pans around, then bake for 5 to 10 minutes more, until golden, well risen, and springy to the touch. Do not over-bake or buns will be dry.

10 Serve buns warm. Best eaten the same day, though leftovers will keep in the fridge for a couple of days.

STEP 5

STEP 6

STEP 9

SAMBAL HAYBEE

MAKES ABOUT 2 CUPS SAMBAL

INGREDIENTS

70 g	tamarind pulp
150 g	water
150 g	dried shrimp (haybee)
4	fresh red chillies, deseeded if desired
80 g	purple shallots, peeled and chopped
30 g	garlic, sliced and peeled
½ tsp	belacan (fermented shrimp paste)
4	candlenuts or cashew nuts
50 g	lemongrass, thinly sliced
50 g	galangal, peeled and finely chopped
2 tsp	finely chopped peeled fresh turmeric
4 tbsp	sunflower oil
3 tbsp	white or brown sugar, plus additional for adjusting
4	kaffir lime leaves, roughly torn
	salt (optional)

EQUIPMENT

- a food processor or blender

METHOD

1 Knead tamarind pulp and water together until the pulp dissolves. Strain out and discard seeds and fibres. Set tamarind liquid aside.

2 Wipe any dust off dried shrimp with slightly damp paper towels. Pulse-blend dried shrimp in small batches in a food processor or blender, until it breaks up and fluffs up into a fine, light floss (haybee and floss pictured at lower left). Set aside.

3 No need to clean the processor—go on to grind chillies, shallots, garlic, belacan, candlenuts, lemongrass, galangal and turmeric together into a very fine paste.

4 Set a wok or heavy-based pan over medium-high heat. When very hot, swirl in oil, then add spice paste and fry vigorously for 5 to 6 minutes, until thickened and darkened, and the oil begins to seep out again.

5 Add sugar to wok and fry for 30 seconds, then add tamarind liquid and fry for 30 seconds more. Add shrimp floss and lime leaves. Reduce heat to medium-low and fry, stirring constantly, for 15 to 20 minutes. The sambal is done when it has separated into small moist clumps, smells a bit caramelised, and the lime leaves have become slightly wizened and dry.

6 Taste and adjust seasoning with more sugar or salt as needed, then fry for several seconds more to disperse the seasoning. Let sambal cool completely before storing.

POINTERS

- Asian supermarkets and dry-goods stores sell belacan in blocks or flat cakes—Thai types may come in small screw-top jars. Keep it in a cool place or the fridge, double-bagged and in an absolutely airtight container.
- If you want to keep the sambal for longer periods, cook it a bit drier; but, it should fall more on the moist side for making pani popo.
- The lime leaves should crumble into small edible fragments during the cooking. If not, pick them out before eating.
- Store sambal in a resealable bag with the air pressed out, tucked into an airtight container. It will keep for at least 3 weeks in the fridge, at least 2 months in the freezer.

Whole and ground-up dried shrimp.

THINKING CAPS

Before I decided that people were more interesting than plants, and correspondingly got a psych degree, I spent several years yearning to be some sort of biologist.

I've spent some of my happiest hours rambling around wild or semi-wild places, observing trees and animals. And fungi—I don't regularly forage for food (unless you count forgotten corners of my fridge), but I do gather photos of random mushrooms I spot along road verges and in parks. Fungi are boundlessly weird. They spring up quietly and overnight; they can smell of almonds or musk or caramel or spices; they can look like ears or lace or furry animals or humongous eggs; the world's largest organism is a fungus occupying a few square miles of turf.

There are of course many recipes for baked fungi, but baked goods that merely (and marvellously) look like them are just as diverting. The first recipe that follows is the happy offspring of a Turkish shaping technique, a Malay-style melt-in-the-mouth suji biskut dough, and Italian white truffle oil—out of all the cookies I bake, this one has made the most people go "Huh?"

MAKES 25 TO 30 COOKIES

INGREDIENTS

190 g	plain flour
110 g	cornstarch
100 g	icing sugar
½ tsp	double-acting baking powder
½ tsp	fine salt
1 tsp	water
140 g	unsalted butter, softened until spreadable
2½ tbsp	hazelnut oil
1 tbsp	cocoa powder, sifted
	white truffle oil, for careful drizzling

EQUIPMENT

- a baking sheet lined with baking paper
- an empty glass bottle (see pointers)

POINTERS

- The glass bottle I use has a mouth about 2.5 cm wide, and a lip about 4 mm thick all round.
- Despite being named for the suji (semolina) they traditionally contain, many suji biskut recipes use only regular wheat flour for a finer, smoother result.

WHITE TRUFFLE BUTTONS

I learnt this shaping method from a great book called *Turkish Bakery Delight*, by Deniz Göktürk Akçakanat. White truffle oil—which is mostly artificially aromatised and has rarely been near a truffle—has suffered from overuse (can you say 'bistronomy'?), but it does have its moments. Here, it harmonises with the hazelnut oil to extend the fungal fantasy.

METHOD

1 Sift flour, cornstarch, icing sugar and baking powder through a fine sieve into a bowl. Whisk for 1 full minute until thoroughly combined.

2 In a mixing bowl, dissolve the salt in the water. Add butter and hazelnut oil, and work the ingredients together with a spatula until well combined and completely smooth.

3 Add dry ingredients to butter-oil mixture and stir slowly—the mixture will start out dry and crumbly, but will eventually come together into a silky dough. Knead briefly until it coheres into a ball, then wrap in plastic wrap and chill for at least 3 hours.

4 Preheat oven to 160°C. Place a shelf in the middle position.

5 Unwrap the dough and divide it into pieces of about 22 to 25 g each. Working swiftly but smoothly, squish and roll each piece between your palms into a round ball that has an even texture throughout, with no colder, harder zones in it. This helps the cookies bake evenly. Space the balls out on the baking sheet, about 3 cm apart.

6 Place cocoa powder in a small bowl. Dip the mouth of the glass bottle into the cocoa powder, then press it gently but decisively downwards into a dough ball, flattening it slightly to form the mushroom shape. Lift it off the dough *without twisting it*. Shape remaining cookies likewise.

7 Bake the cookies for 15 to 18 minutes, until slightly puffed and pale golden. Transfer sheets to racks to cool.

8 As soon as the cookies have reached room temperature, drip 2 to 3 drops of white truffle oil on each one, and let it soak in. Don't overdo it—this stuff is powerful. Place each cookie—they are fragile—in a paper cupcake case, and nestle these in an airtight container. Store in the fridge.

8 The cookies start out crisp, slowly becoming melt-in-the-mouth by the third or fourth day after baking. They are best eaten within a week.

CHOCOLATE CHEESECAKE SHIITAKE 'SHROOMS

With button mushrooms under my belt (figuratively speaking), I had to add a shiitake-shaped cookie to my repertoire too. It took me two years of intermittent experiments to work out how to make these craze and crack just like the real thing. For maximum viewing enjoyment, tell people the name of these cookies first, then serve them, and watch their faces. Soft and slightly chewy, they taste like a white chocolate cheesecake with a cocoa wafer crust.

MAKES 30 TO 34 COOKIES

INGREDIENTS

Dough

100 g	plain flour
90 g	cake flour
1 tsp	double-acting baking powder
⅛ tsp	bicarbonate of soda
120 g	white chocolate, finely chopped
80 g	cold unsalted butter, cubed
60 g	cream cheese
95 g	fine suger
¼ tsp	fine salt
2 tsp	vanilla extract
1 tsp	lemon extract
1	egg
2 tsp	lemon juice

For coating

150 g	granulated or fine white sugar, approximately
6 tbsp	cocoa powder
2 tsp	potato starch

EQUIPMENT

- a cake mixer fitted with the paddle attachment, or a sturdy spatula and a strong arm
- a baking sheet lined with baking paper

METHOD

1 Sift plain flour, cake flour, baking powder and bicarbonate of soda into a bowl, and whisk very well to mix. Set aside.

2 Place white chocolate in a heatproof bowl and set it over a small pan of barely simmering water—it should completely cover the pan, so water cannot splash into the chocolate. Stir occasionally until the chocolate melts. Take the bowl off the pan and set it aside.

3 In a mixing bowl, cream butter, cream cheese, sugar, salt, and both extracts together until well blended and fluffy. Beat in the egg and lemon juice until thoroughly blended, then scrape in the white chocolate and beat until smooth and incorporated. Fold in dry ingredients to make a soft, even dough. Cover bowl and let dough stand at cool room temperature (or in the fridge if it's a hot day) for 20 minutes.

4 Preheat oven to 170°C. Place a shelf in the middle position.

5 Set out your coating ingredients. Place the white sugar in a shallow dish. Sift the cocoa powder and potato starch together into another shallow dish.

6 Scoop a scant 1-tablespoon amount of dough and drop it into the white sugar. Roll it until it is thoroughly coated with sugar, then quickly roll it between your palms to make it evenly spherical. Drop it into the cocoa powder dish and roll to coat lightly but evenly, then lift it out and place on the baking sheet. Make remaining cookies likewise.

7 Bake the cookies for 12 to 13 minutes, until puffed and cracked. Transfer sheet to a rack. As soon as cookies are cool, transfer them to an airtight container. Shrooms will keep, refrigerated, for 3 to 4 days.

POINTERS

- You can use either Dutch-processed (my preference, page 16) or natural cocoa powder. The darker cookies in the photo were made with the former, the paler ones with the latter.
- For the most well defined cracks, shape and bake only one sheet of cookies at a time. Keep the remaining dough at cool room temperature or in the fridge in the meantime.

5.

TOOLS & GADGETS

Interior—a small, nondescript room. Tired faces. The faint smell of sugar.

Hi... my name is Chris, and...and...I'm a bakeware addict.

Oh wow that was a loud hello. Strong coffee, huh?

So, how it started... When I was a kid I got birthday cakes in all kinds of shapes...rabbits...elephants...Spider-man was a good one, my tongue was blue for hours after... So maybe that, uh, primed the pump. When I was 10, I found an old Wilton catalogue with photos of cakes shaped like beer mugs and furry lions...one even had a little tiered fountain which ran with real water... I read it over and over until all the pages were scuffed.

For years I kept my compulsions under control. Then I started working and could afford to buy stuff. I began hoarding loaf tins in all sizes. I'd be rummaging in a drawer and find a complicated cookie doodad that I didn't even recall buying... and then another, and another. It escalated from there.

When...when I travel overseas for work, I map out routes from my hotel to bakeries and baking shops. I bring an extra check-in bag, and containers for pastries, and I never forget bubble wrap, not since the time I did and then had to stuff a pandoro mould with socks so it wouldn't distort.

The biggest heaviest thing I've lugged home? Uh, a three-litre limited edition cast aluminium bundt pan, from the US. It was so curvy...so inviting.

I try to avoid baking supply shops and department store kitchen sections near ATM machines. It's just too risky. I stay at home during festive sales, but it's so hard...it's just so hard. They call to me, you see. I hear them calling. It's like a ringing noise. Like bells.

Thank you, thank you all for your kind support. And for listening...it, it means a lot to me that you would listen.

What's that?

Um...okay. Sure, I can bring some cake next week.

What shape would you like?

SUSPENSEFUL

As an accumulator of old cookbooks, I have become at home with odd culinary locutions. ‘One chittack and a half of ghee’, ‘Lardaceous Sponge Cake’, ‘fry rice deliciously’, ‘stretch the pig’s omentum over the table’, ‘3 cents bean paste’ and such. I thought I’d seen it all.

However. In a vintage Taiwanese book titled *International Baking Delights*, I came across in the equipment glossary a photo of a four-pronged wire-thing like a gangly trivet, labelled ‘cake hanger’. Next to it were a ‘rubber specular’, a ‘flowering mouth tube’ and a ‘doughnut mode’.

This last was a ring mould, the mouth tube was a star piping tip, and you can probably guess what the specular was, but 'cake hanger'? A torture device for badly-behaved desserts? Leaving the suspense unresolved, the book failed to mention the cake hanger anywhere beyond the glossary, though it did include a host of enigmatically named recipes, such as Rolls With Scaly Crust, Filled Pastry Deltas, and Oriental Surprises.

I found closure in another book years afterwards: a cake hanger helps you produce cakes too fragile to hold up their own weight while fresh and hot.

Such a cake is baked in an ungreased loose-based pan, so it sticks to it all round. The cake hanger is inserted into the cake; and the whole assembly inverted, the hanger's legs pressing the pan base against its confining rim. The cake hangs, suspended from the pan sides and base, as it cools and sets into air-pocketed sponginess.

This is exactly how a chiffon cake cools in its inverted ring mould—except that, with a cake hanger, you can bake a chiffon or chiffon-light cake in nearly any pan, as long as it has a loose base. How Taiwanese bakers have kept this a secret from most of the developed baking world—or at least home bakers—for so long is baffling. Perhaps the genius idea was lost in translation.

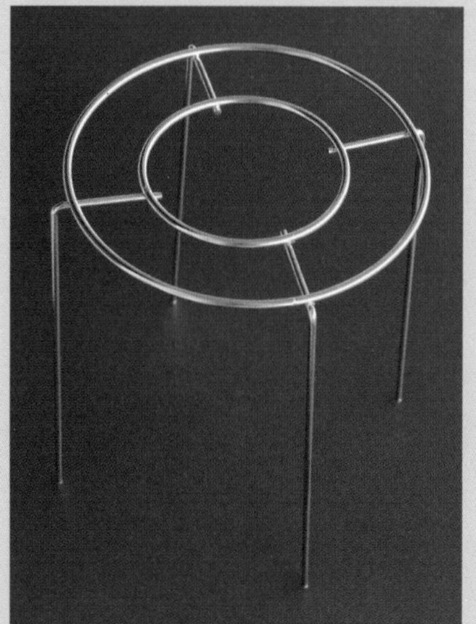

Cake hangers can be found at baking supply shops selling Taiwanese bakeware, or bought online. You could also MacGyver your own version by sticking 4 or 5 long, sturdy wooden skewers into a block of dense styrofoam or florist foam, flat ends sticking out.

SOFTLY-SOFTLY CHOCOLATE CAKE

I love the lightness of chiffon cake, which is normally made with oil, but I also love the union of chocolate and butter. The cake hanger allows me to enjoy both simultaneously. At first bite, this cake seems like a chiffon, with a light, fine and tender crumb. Then, as it falls apart and unfurls its flavour, it tastes fudgier, almost brownie-like...and then it disappears with a final bittersweet kiss.

SERVES 8 TO 12

INGREDIENTS

60 g	plain flour
35 g	cake flour
10 g	cornstarch
100 g	water
50 g	unsalted butter
45 g	light muscovado sugar
¼ tsp	salt
25 g	cocoa powder
95 g	dark chocolate, 60 to 70 per cent cacao, finely chopped
30 g	sunflower oil
1 tsp	vanilla extract
5	egg whites
⅔ tsp	cream of tartar
100 g	caster sugar
5	egg yolks
1 tbsp	rum
	whipped cream, to serve

EQUIPMENT

- a round cake tin with a removable base, 20 or 21 cm in diameter and at least 6 cm deep, dry and ungreased

METHOD

1 Preheat oven to 160°C. Place a shelf in the middle position.

2 Sift plain flour, cake flour and cornstarch into a bowl. Whisk to blend thoroughly. Set aside.

3 Combine water, butter, muscovado sugar and salt in a small pot. Cover and cook over low heat until the butter has melted and the mixture is nearing a simmer. Take pot off the heat, uncover it, and whisk in the cocoa powder until smooth. Add chocolate, oil and vanilla, and stir with the whisk until the chocolate has melted and the mixture is glossy and smooth. Scrape it into a mixing bowl and let it cool to barely lukewarm.

4 In a clean, grease-free bowl, beat egg whites with cream of tartar until soft peaks form, then gradually beat in caster sugar. Beat until stiff, glossy, snow-white peaks just start to form—do not over-beat. Set the meringue aside momentarily.

5 Add egg yolks and rum to chocolate mixture and whisk to blend thoroughly, then add flour mixture and whisk until smooth. The batter will be fairly thick.

6 Fold one-third of the meringue into the batter until almost blended, then fold in half the remaining meringue. Finally, scrape the batter into the meringue bowl and fold to incorporate the remaining meringue. Scrape mixture into the cake tin.

7 Bake for 40 to 45 minutes. It will dome and may crack during baking—this is normal. It is done when a tester inserted in its centre emerges clean.

8 Remove the cake from the oven, insert the cake hanger, and swiftly invert it onto a tray (page 234). Let cool completely. It will shrink slightly as it cools, its top reverting to flatness.

9 To unmould, turn the cake right side up and remove the cake hanger. Run a thin, sharp knife around its edge, and remove the tin sides. Run the knife around the cake's base to detach it from the tin base, and slide it onto a serving plate.

10 Top with whipped cream—I swirl it with a spoon, or pipe it in slightly demented random loops, curls or the Marcel waves shown here. Slice to serve.

POINTERS

- I prefer regular Dutch-processed cocoa powder (page 16) for this cake.
- A finely milled, slightly soft plain flour, around 9 to 10 percent protein—such as Italian 00—works best in this cake.
- Before serving it, I rest this cake for 24 hours in a covered container, so that it absorbs moisture from the air and becomes even softer—but then, I live in a very humid country. Alternatively, moisten it with liquor or a very light syrup.
- Another serving suggestion: split the cake in half, sprinkle the halves lightly with liquor, syrup or coffee, then sandwich them together with stiffly whipped cream. Cover and chill for 2 hours before serving.

COOKIE SMARTS

I love a good browse around a Peranakan museum or heritage house, bursting at the seams with epergnes and embroidery and mother-of-pearl inlay, but I couldn't live with that kind of décor. White walls and wood grain à la the Scandinavians and Shakers are much more my thing; I'd always thought the Peranakan gene for love of ornamentation had passed me by.

That is, until the day I was tidying my equipment cupboard and realised how many cookie cutters I'd amassed. And stamps. And pincers. And presses. And Chinese piah* moulds. And other unnamed widgets for shaping intricate biscuity type things. Such is destiny.

**'Piah' in Mandarin dialect can mean cake or biscuit or cookie—something small and baked.*

Clockwise from far left, top: *pineapple cake frames; stamping pineapple-strawberry shortcakes; a snowflake cookie cutter; brass and wood pineapple tart cutters; an Indonesian cacao pod-shaped cookie mould; a Filipino polvoron cookie press.*

PINEAPPLE-STRAWBERRY SHORTCAKES

MAKES ABOUT 20 CAKES

INGREDIENTS

Jam

160 g	hulled and trimmed fresh strawberries
⅛	lemon, zest, pith and all
340 g	sugar
600 g	fresh pineapple, cored and chopped

Pastry

250 g	plain flour
50 g	cornstarch
2 tsp	milk powder
35 g	icing sugar
¼ tsp	fine salt
200 g	cold salted butter, cut into small cubes, plus additional for greasing
2	egg yolks
50 g	cream cheese, softened
½ tsp	vanilla extract
	rice flour, for dusting

EQUIPMENT

- a food processor or blender
- a large, heavy-based frying pan, preferably non-stick
- a stand mixer fitted with the paddle attachment
- a baking sheet lined with baking paper
- square pineapple cake frames
- cookie or mooncake press stamps, if desired

The history of pineapple pastries in Asia is a chequered, and crimped, and pinched one. The tale of how and where a South American fruit first coupled with Dutch dough is lost in the mists of unrecorded history, but their offspring now spangle Southeast Asia like stars, baked by many communities—Eurasian, Peranakan, Chinese, Malay—and in many shapes.

This recipe is based on a typical Taiwanese pineapple shortcake, which encases sweet pineapple-winter melon jam in a rich pastry dosed with powdered milk for a fine, friable texture. Good ones are sublime; bad ones smell of marker pens and industrial cheese. I add strawberry and lemon to the pineapple, for a tart and lively contrast to shells of buttery cream cheese shortcrust shells.

Pineapple cake frames are small aluminium rings, thicker but lighter than regular tart rings or tins. They come in different shapes, but among the easiest to find and use are 5 cm square frames, sold singly or in connected strips, as shown on the previous page.

METHOD

1 Make the jam. Dice strawberries. Finely mince lemon—zest, pith, flesh and all—and combine it with strawberries and sugar in a glass or stainless steel bowl. Cover and set aside.

2 Pulse-blend pineapple in a food processor or blender to a medium-coarse puree, not completely smooth; you want a little texture left in it. Scrape puree into a large frying pan and set over medium-high heat. Bring it to the boil, then cook, stirring constantly with a heatproof spatula and scraping the pan bottom, until it has reduced to about half of its original volume, and has become very thick. This should take 15 to 20 minutes.

3 Add the contents of the strawberry bowl to the pan. Cook, stirring constantly, for another 30 minutes or so, give or take a few minutes, until it has become a glossy, brick-red paste, like a very thick chutney. Reduce the heat as it thickens so it won't burn or scorch.

4 Scrape the jam into a clean bowl and let it cool completely, then transfer it to a clean airtight container and chill it until it is firm. You should have about 400 g.

5 Make the pastry. Sift flour, cornstarch, milk powder and icing sugar into a mixing bowl, add salt and whisk to blend thoroughly. Add butter to the bowl, and mix on low speed for about 2 minutes, until butter is fully dispersed and the mixture looks sandy.

6 In a small bowl, whisk egg yolk, cream cheese and vanilla together until smooth, then scrape mixture into the mixing bowl. Mix on low speed until dough comes together

into a rough ball. Wrap dough in plastic wrap and chill for at least 8 hours.

7 Preheat oven to 165°C. Place a shelf in the middle position.

8 Place pineapple cake frames on the paper-lined baking sheets. Grease the inside of each frame with butter. Divide dough into 30 g portions and jam into 25 g portions. Roll all of them into balls.

9 Dust your hands well with rice flour. With your hands, flatten a ball of dough to about 3 cm thickness. Place a jam ball on top, bring up edges of dough to enclose jam, and pinch well to seal. Pat the parcel into a frame, easing it into the corners, then flatten its top either with your fingertips, or with a cookie or mooncake stamp lightly dusted with rice flour. Here I have used a small square one (shown on page 243) that just fits inside the frame. Make all shortcakes likewise.

10 Bake the shortcakes for 21 to 24 minutes, until golden. Transfer baking sheet to a rack, let cakes stand for 5 minutes, then run a small, thin knife blade around the edge of each shortcake, so you can later lift off the frames more easily. Let cool until lukewarm, then lift off frames. The shortcakes keep for at least 2 weeks in an airtight container in the fridge.

POINTERS

- Make the jam in the biggest frying pan you have—it will reduce faster and retain more of the fruits' subtleties. Do not overcook the jam, or it will set rock-hard. When done, it will look soft while hot and in the pan, but will firm up into malleability when cool.
- For the best results, bake the cookies one sheet at a time, in batches if necessary. Wipe out and re-grease the shortcake frames between batches.

PISTACHIO BUTTER CARRÉS

In 1980s London, small minimarts in my 'hood sold snacks and goodies from different parts of Europe. I especially loved Dutch kanos, pastry 'canoes' stuffed with almond paste or almond cream. Plain and homely-looking, they dissolved divinely into fragrant, buttery crumbs in the mouth. This is my pistachio-ed homage to Holland, which I bake in pineapple cake frames and hence call carrés after their square shape.

MAKES 12 COOKIES

INGREDIENTS

Dough

200 g	plain flour
20 g	potato starch
1 tsp	double-acting baking powder
80 g	caster sugar
½ tsp	fine salt
140 g	cold unsalted butter, cubed, plus additional for greasing
1 tbsp	pistachio paste (see pointers)
½ tsp	vanilla extract

Filling

35 g	finely ground skinned pistachio nuts
30 g	caster sugar
¼ tsp	cornstarch
30 g	unsalted butter, softened until spreadable
½	a beaten egg

EQUIPMENT

- a stand mixer fitted with the paddle attachment
- square pineapple cake frames
- a baking sheet lined with baking paper

STEP 5

METHOD

1 Make dough. Sift flour, potato starch and baking powder into a mixing bowl. Add sugar and salt and beat on low speed until thoroughly blended, about 1 minute.

2 While beating continuously on low speed, add butter to bowl. Beat for about 1 to 2 minutes, until butter disperses and the dough looks like damp, clumpy sand. Stop beating and drizzle pistachio paste and vanilla over dough. Mix on low speed until dough comes together into a ball. Wrap dough in plastic wrap and chill for 1 to 2 hours.

3 Make the filling. Whisk pistachios, sugar and cornstarch together in a small mixing bowl. With a spatula, work in the butter until blended, then add the egg and beat until smooth. Cover and chill until needed.

4 Preheat oven to 175°C. Place a shelf in the middle position.

5 Place pineapple cake frames on the paper-lined baking sheet. Grease the inside of each frame with butter. Divide dough into 12 portions. Take 1 portion and split it into two slightly unequal halves. Press the larger half into a pineapple cake frame, so it covers the bottom and spreads a little up the sides, forming a hollow in the middle. Pipe a dab of filling into the hollow. Flatten the other half of the dough into a thin square, place on top of the filling, and press the edges to seal. Make all cakes likewise.

6 Bake the carrés for 16 to 18 minutes, until deep golden. They will rise a little during baking.

7 Transfer baking sheet to a rack. Let carrés stand for 5 minutes, then run a small, thin knife blade around the edges of each carré, so you can later lift off the moulds more easily. Let cool for 10 minutes more, then lift off moulds.

8 Serving these warm from the oven heightens the knee-weakeningly wonderful contrast between crisp shell and soft interior. Resting them for a day or two after baking, in an airtight container at cool room temperature, lets them attain a mellow softness that is both moist and crumbly.

POINTERS

- If you can't get pistachio paste, which is a very smooth, very green pistachio puree sold at baking supply shops, use an egg yolk or a tablespoon of cream instead.

MAKES 18 TO 20 SANDWICH COOKIES

INGREDIENTS

Dough

190 g	cake flour
150 g	icing sugar
80 g	cocoa powder (see pointers)
25 g	cornstarch
25 g	rice flour
200 g	cold unsalted butter, diced
1 tbsp	water
1½ tsp	vanilla extract
⅓ tsp	fine salt

Filling

1 recipe	custard cream filling (page 70)
2½ tsp	matcha powder
2 tsp	hot water

For dusting

1 tbsp	rice flour
1 tbsp	cocoa powder

EQUIPMENT

- a stand mixer fitted with the paddle attachment
- baking sheets lined with baking paper
- cookie stamps

CHOCOLATE MATCHA SANDWICH COOKIES

I'm not really a fan of commercial chocolate sandwich cookies—the highly alkalised extra-dark cocoa they're gothed up with makes them look (and almost taste) like compost. Except this one time in a supermarket, when limited edition made-in-Japan Matcha Oreos called out to me in high, kawaii voices. I bought them, sampled one, then almost finished the entire packet in one go. They never appeared again, so I figured out my own version. The dusky dough is very cocoa-y, not too sweet, and retains stamped detail beautifully.

METHOD

1 Sift cake flour, icing sugar, cocoa powder, cornstarch and rice flour into a mixing bowl. Beat until well blended. Add butter to bowl and beat continuously on low speed for 1 to 2 minutes, until it disperses. When the dough starts to darken and clump together in coarse crumbs, stop beating.

2 Whisk water, vanilla and salt together until salt dissolves, then drizzle mixture over dough crumbs. Mix on low speed until dough coheres into a soft ball. Stop beating, and knead dough briefly with your hands to even it out. Wrap dough in plastic wrap and chill for at least 6 hours or overnight.

3 Make up the custard cream filling (page 70). Whisk matcha and hot water together into a smooth paste, let it cool, and beat it into the filling. Cover and chill matcha filling until needed.

4 Preheat oven to 180°C. Place a shelf in the middle position. Sift dusting ingredients together into a small bowl.

5 Divide the dough into portions of 16 to 20 g each. Roll them into balls between your palms, but don't let them soften too much.

6 Coat a ball lightly but evenly in the dusting mixture, and place it on the baking sheet. Flatten it with a cookie stamp into a disc about 2 to 3 mm thick. Repeat with remaining dough, spacing cookies about 2 cm apart.

7 Bake the cookies for 16 to 18 minutes. They don't change in size or colour much—you can sacrifice one to check if it's cooked through to the middle. When done but still hot, they are fragile and soft, but firm up as they cool. Transfer baking sheet to a rack and let cookies stand undisturbed until completely cooled.

8 Spread or pipe the filling on the flat bottoms of half the cookies, then top with remaining cookies, patterned sides up. Keep chilled in an airtight container until serving time.

POINTERS

- Use regular Dutch-processed cocoa powder. Extra-dark cocoa makes bitter, soapy cookies.
- The dusting mixture stops the dough sticking to the cookie stamp. I use heavy plastic stamps (shown above) originally meant for Korean tteok, or rice cakes. You can use any kind of pattern-impressing implement: a cut-glass tumbler base, or fondant-embossing tools, or the sole of a newly unboxed designer sneaker, and such.
- Bake one tray of cookies at a time for the most even results. Dust and stamp them only just before baking.

VAPOUR SCULPTURE

My friends make fun of how I smell my food, leaning low over each plate and inhaling deeply to catch every last tendril of wok hei ('wok breath'—not a Chinese gangsta insult, but the unfakeable fragrance resulting from oils, proteins and carbs colliding with superheated metal). Just as a cologne's top notes dissipate within minutes of being applied, the scent of a good dish lasts for mere moments, and I don't like to miss them.

Which is why tian op immediately intrigued me when I first learned of them. Double-ended Thai beeswax candles, they are infused with aromatics which may include sandalwood, camphor, patchouli,

benzoin resin, kaffir lime zest and frankincense. They are lit, snuffed, placed in a container with cookies or desserts, or ingredients like coconut milk or plain water, and the whole tightly covered so that the trapped candle smoke suffuses the items.

It's not as strange as it may sound. Things that taste good, things that smell good, and things that burn well have long and intertwined histories. Much like tian op, a northern Indian technique called dhungar permeates dishes with trapped smoke from a live coal sprinkled with ghee and spices. American southern barbecue is all about the long, slow and smoky cooking of meat on an enclosed grill.

A few years after hearing about tian op, I finally obtained some, thanks to Bangkok-visiting friends willing to be candle mules. The initial smoke wafts were quite powerful, like a 1980s oriental perfume advertised with menacing-looking ladies.

The traces they left in the food were more subtle, a beguiling and completely unexpected synthesis of the hot tea, rice pudding, incense-like parquet wax and sharpened pencils of my English schooldays.

If you cannot get tian op (left, top), look in Thai grocery stores for candle-infused coconut cream—two brands are shown here (left, bottom)—and use this instead of regular coconut cream in the cookie dough.

SMOKED CLOUD COOKIES

This Indonesian-style kue semprit dough, a descendant of Dutch spritskoekjes, blends tapioca starch with soft wheat flour for an especially fine, delicate texture, which also absorbs the smoke well.

MAKES ABOUT 22 TO 26 COOKIES

INGREDIENTS

150 g	cake flour
30 g	tapioca starch
70 g	icing sugar
125 g	unsalted butter, cubed and softened until just spreadable
25 g	coconut cream
⅛ tsp	fine salt

EQUIPMENT

- a baking sheet lined with baking paper
- a piping bag fitted with a 7mm closed-star piping tip
- one tian op smoking candle

POINTERS

- You can line the inside of the container lid with foil so that it won't get soot-stained before the candle goes out.
- Some online stores sell tian op. If you're travelling to Bangkok or other large Thai cities, look for them in wet markets or supermarkets—I even saw them in a Thai Tesco once.

METHOD

1 Preheat oven to 170°C. Place a shelf in the middle position.

2 With a very fine sieve, sift cake flour, tapioca starch and icing sugar together twice, then whisk well to blend.

3 Combine the butter, coconut cream and salt in a mixing bowl, and work them together with a spatula until evenly blended. Add flour mixture and fold in until the dough is smooth and even.

4 Spoon the dough into piping bag. Twist bag to seal. Pipe free-form swirly cloud shapes onto the baking sheet, making them about 5 to 6 cm across and spacing them about 3 cm apart.

5 Bake the cookies for 13 to 15 minutes, until touched with colour and cooked through. Transfer baking sheet to a rack to cool. As soon as they are cool and have firmed up, transfer them to an airtight container. Smoke them within a few hours of being baked, for the best results.

6 To smoke the cookies, take a large, deep container with a lid, preferably porcelain or glass. In its centre place an upturned egg cup, shot glass, or something that will elevate the smoking candle above the container's base. Arrange the cookies around the egg cup.

7 Trim off any blackened wick from previous uses of the tian op. Light both wicks, and place the candle on the egg cup. Cover the container. Within seconds, the candle should burn up the remaining oxygen in the container, and go out, emitting plumes of smoke. This is fun to watch. Leave the container undisturbed for about 30 minutes or so. If you want the cookies to smell stronger, leave them for longer, or repeat the lighting, snuffing and steeping one or more times.

8 When the cookies are scented enough for your liking, open the container and transfer them to a clean airtight vessel. Wash the container. Wrap up the candle and stash it in an airtight jar in a cool place for the next use.

RING LEADER

I like bundt cakes. I like just saying the word bundt. Bundt bundt bundt.

Bundt pans and the cakes baked therein are tall and ring-shaped, and descend from similarly toroidal traditional European cakes and cake-breads.

The original cast-aluminium bundt pan was designed, and its name (not a real noun) coined and trademarked, by America's Nordic Ware company in the 1950s. That simple, voluptuous, kugelhopf-inspired design has now been joined by many beautiful and rococo siblings, some of which I own, many more of which I covet quite unnecessarily.

Bundt cakes are often decadent, invariably decorative, and able to feed a crowd and make them happy. They are fun. They are *fundt*.

GINGERBREAD FUDGE BUNDT CAKE

SERVES 12 TO 16

INGREDIENTS

Fudge filling

95 g	dark chocolate, at least 65 per cent cacao, finely chopped
12 g	cornstarch
10 g	cocoa powder
35 g	muscovado sugar
115 g	water
115 g	cream

Cake batter

125 g	cake flour
125 g	wholewheat pastry flour (page 14)
25 g	potato starch
¾ tsp	double-acting baking powder
⅓ tsp	bicarbonate of soda
4 tsp	ground ginger
1 tsp	ground cinnamon
½ tsp	ground nutmeg
½ tsp	ground cardamom
200 g	unsalted butter, slightly softened
100 g	cream cheese
200 g	light muscovado sugar
80 g	caster sugar
1 tsp	vanilla extract
½ tsp	lemon extract
¼ tsp	salt
3	egg yolks
150 g	plain unsweetened yoghurt, preferably Greek-style
3	egg whites
	butter and flour, or oil-and-flour spray, for preparing pan
	icing sugar, for dusting

EQUIPMENT

- a stand mixer fitted with the paddle attachment
- a 3-litre capacity bundt pan or ring mould, greased well and floured, or sprayed with oil-and-flour baking spray

The cake which famously put the bundt pan on the map was the Tunnel of Fudge, entered in the 1966 Pillsbury Bake-Off competition by a baker named Ella Helfrich. Nut-studded and gooey-middled, it came in second, pipped weirdly at the post by a bread concocted with processed cheese spread and dry onion soup mix. The real winner, however, was inarguably Nordic Ware, which was subsequently deluged with pan orders from Ella-fans.

I was very curious about the Tunnel, until I found out the reason for its soft centre: *the batter contains so much sugar that it is unable to fully set*. Stop and consider that for a second. Yup. Not something a pancreas would enjoy. That killed my interest in the cake—but not the concept. Some time afterwards, saddled with leftover chocolate pudding from a recipe testing bout, I suddenly remembered the Tunnel, and the rest was kismet.

In my recipe, the cake is a fine-grained, pale blond gingerbread with aromatic spice accents and a good kick of ginger, the better to contrast with a creamy, bittersweet chocolate core. It takes some advance planning, but is no more difficult to make than a regular frosted bundt cake. And I mean, come on, *cake with a frosting baked inside*.

METHOD

1 Make the fudge filling the day before. Place chocolate in a heatproof bowl, and set aside. Sift cornstarch and cocoa powder into a small pot, then whisk in muscovado sugar to blend. Slowly whisk in water, followed by cream. Set pot over medium-low heat and cook, whisking constantly, until mixture comes to a full simmer, with many little blooping bubbles, and thickens. Scrape mixture into the bowl with the chocolate, wait 10 seconds, then stir slowly until chocolate has melted and mixture is smooth. Place bowl in a larger bowl of cold water and cool filling to room temperature. Cover it with plastic wrap, pressing it against the filling's surface, and chill overnight, until completely cold.

2 Preheat oven to 180°C. Have your pan ready. Place a shelf in the middle position.

3 Sift both flours, potato starch, baking powder and bicarbonate of soda into a bowl. Add ground spices and whisk to blend very thoroughly.

4 Beat butter and cream cheese together on medium-low speed until smooth, and no lumps of either remain. Add both sugars, both extracts, and salt, and beat on medium-high speed for 2 to 3 minutes, until light and fluffy. Beat in egg yolks one at a time.

(continued on the next page)

STEP 1

STEP 6

STEP 6

POINTERS

- Take the time to grease-and-flour, or spray, every nook and cranny of your bundt pan as evenly as you can, and the cake will release with no problems.
- Be methodical in step 6. Any trapped air may show up later as empty pockets in the tunnel—it won't affect the texture of the cake, but may look a bit awkward.
- Keep leftovers refrigerated, in an airtight container. Finish the cake within a couple of days, as the moist centre makes it perishable.
- Bundt pans are made out of thin stamped metal or thick cast metal. Thicker pans are more expensive but worth the investment, lasting a lifetime if washed by hand and treated gently, and yielding cakes which rise high and have very even crusts.

5 Add flour mixture to bowl. Mix in on lowest speed until barely incorporated and mixture looks crumbly and thick, scraping down bowl sides halfway. Scrape down bowl sides again, then add yoghurt and beat on medium-low speed just until incorporated. Scrape down bowl sides again, add egg whites, and beat for about 30 seconds on medium-low speed, until completely smooth.

6 Spoon two-thirds of the batter into the bundt pan. Tap it on the countertop to settle and level out the batter. With a spoon, 'carve' a ring-shaped trough running down the middle of the batter. Spoon the filling into the trough—it is easiest to put the filling in a piping bag, and then pipe it into the trough. Smooth the surface of the filling with the back of a spoon, to ensure no air is trapped anywhere within it. Spoon and spread the remaining cake batter evenly over the filling, covering it completely from view.

7 Tap pan lightly on the counter to settle batter, then place it on the middle oven shelf. Bake for about 40 minutes, until well risen, deeply browned, and a cake tester inserted into the cake—but not as far as the chocolate centre—emerges damp but clean. Transfer the pan to a rack. It will shrink slightly as it cools.

8 Unmould the completely cooled cake onto a serving plate. Serve it right away, or cover it airtight and chill it slightly. Dust with icing sugar before serving.

MAPLE-MISO BUNDT CAKE

SERVES 10 TO 12

INGREDIENTS

Cake batter

100 g	wholewheat pastry flour (page 14)
130 g	cake flour
20 g	potato starch
¾ tsp	baking powder
¼ tsp	fine salt
160 g	unsalted butter
30 g	cream
45 g	shiro miso (see pointers)
2	eggs
3	egg yolks
175 g	maple syrup (see pointers)
85 g	light brown sugar

Glaze

20 g	unsalted butter
45 g	maple syrup
25 g	shiro miso
75 g	icing sugar
	butter and flour, or oil-and-flour spray, for preparing pan

EQUIPMENT

- a cake mixer fitted with the whisk beater
- a 2.5-litre capacity bundt pan or loaf pan, greased well and floured, or sprayed with oil-and-flour baking spray

I once attended and wrote an article about an after-hours gathering of pastry chefs, an informal regular 'do for catching up and swapping ideas, to which every chef would bring along their latest works-in-progress for sampling and feedback. "Bring one too, for fun!" they said, so I did, and was mortified to see my Mexican milk-soaked torta tres leches sitting like a sullen beige swamp next to exquisite pralines on Lucite plinths, stunning plated desserts and other knock-'em-dead confections.

For some reason, I was invited back to the next one. Its theme was log cakes, and so, bent on redeeming myself, I dreamt up two tree-inspired recipes. One was meant to evoke resiny evergreens—infused with rosemary, galangal and lemon, it had a rosemary meringue crust flavoured with Finnish pine tar syrup. It tasted not unlike pricey salon herbal shampoo. The other was a whole-wheat miso-maple-almond pound cake wrapped in miso-maple-almond marzipan, striated to resemble bark—delicious, but earnest and brown, like 1970s hippie food. Both were fragrant with Eau de Trying Too Hard.

I felt, though, that within the madness was salvageable beauty. So I set out to make-over tree #2, after reading about American chef Joanne Chang's method of mixing a pound cake batter as if it were a genoise sponge. I adapted the unorthodox technique to transform hippie lumpenness into a feathery, fluffy swan. Salted caramel macarons, imma let you finish, but this cake formerly known as tree is one of the best savoury sweets of all time.

POINTERS

- Shiro miso literally translates as 'white miso', but the name covers a gamut of miso hues, ranging from ivory to manila-envelope. For this cake I prefer a light yellow, medium-salty shiro miso (pictured, left). If you can only get a strongly salty miso, reduce its quantity in the cake to 40 g and in the glaze to 15 g.
- Use a good medium-dark to dark maple syrup—formerly labelled Grade B or C if Canadian, or Grade B if American, this is nowadays increasingly called Grade A Dark. Lighter syrups aren't sufficiently strong-flavoured.
- This cake tastes best one or two days after baking. Keep it in an airtight container in the fridge, and bring it to room temperature before glazing and serving. As it sits, the respectively nutty, fragrant and funky characters of the whole wheat, maple and miso meld into a subtle earthiness—very Japanese, in a way—layered with hints of butterscotch and salt.

METHOD

1 Preheat oven to 180°C. Grease and flour your pan, or spray it. Place a shelf in the middle position.

2 Sift both flours, potato starch and baking powder into a bowl. Add salt and whisk well to mix.

3 Combine unsalted butter and cream in a heatproof mixing bowl, and set it over a pan of simmering water. When butter has melted, add miso and whisk until smooth. Keep the mixture warm.

4 Combine eggs, egg yolks, maple syrup and brown sugar in a mixing bowl. Beat on medium-high speed until at least tripled in volume and very thick. When lifted clear of the foam, the whisk should trail a thick ribbon that stays on the surface for several seconds before disappearing. This should take at least 5 to 6 minutes with a stand mixer.

5 Add half the flour mixture to the bowl. Detach the whisk beater from the mixer, and, holding it in your hand, use it to fold in the flour until mostly incorporated. Repeat with remaining flour, folding until no large streaks remain.

6 Scrape about a quarter of the batter into the butter mixture, and quickly whisk them together until smooth. Scrape mixture back into the batter bowl, and fold it in, again with the detached whisk beater. Finish up the folding with a large spatula, scraping the bowl's bottom and sides, folding until the batter is smooth and streak-free. It will be heavier than a typical genoise batter but lighter than a pound cake batter.

7 Pour the batter into prepared pan. Bake for 30 to 35 minutes, until risen and well browned, and a cake tester inserted into the cake emerges clean. It should barely start to shrink from the sides of the pan when it is done.

8 Transfer the cake pan to a rack and let cool for about 30 minutes. Carefully unmould the cake onto a serving plate and let it finish cooling.

9 Make the glaze shortly before serving. Combine butter, maple syrup and miso in a pot and stir over low heat until butter melts, then whisk in icing sugar to make a thickly flowing glaze. Pour it evenly over cake—let it drip down the sides attractively, or just sling it in dribs and drabs. Serve immediately, or cover and chill until needed. Slice with a sharp, thin-bladed knife.

ACKNOWLEDGEMENTS

THANKS GO TO

God, who is my beginning • my mum, for being there • my dad, for my education • all the Agapeeps, for the music, the love, and the Pocky • ALOFQ, for being such willing co-eaters, guinea pigs and cheerleaders • the Epigram folks—Edmund, for the opportunity, Sam (remember me when you are famous, k) and Wen Yeu, for all the hard work • Aaron and Namiko, from your manatee in art and life • James, Andrea, Fuchsia and Willin, for the encouragement and empathy • Shermay, for telling me I should teach, all those years ago • all my editors, readers and students, for letting me do what I love to do • and finally God, who is also my ending, and the best bread of all.

PHOTO CREDITS

All photos by Christopher Tan except for:
Cover, Eng Chun Pang
Page 4-5, R. Thomas
Page 9, T. Tan
Page 124-125, B. Pinyowattanacheap
Page 136-137, C.K. Goh
Page 147, top right, G. Ng
Page 272, T. Aspler

INDEX

D.

F.

G.

H.

I.

J.

K.

L.

M.

N.

O.

P.

S.

T.

W.

Y.